THE CONTINENTS

Puzzles for Learning World Geography

Jeanne Cheyney
Arnold Cheyney, Professor Emeritus
University of Miami

Illustrated by Jeanne Cheyney

GoodYearBooks
An Imprint of ScottForesman
A Division of HarperCollins Publishers

Dedication
To our grandson, Jason Arnold Cheyney, for his help in bringing this book
to print

GoodYearBooks

are available for most basic curriculum subjects plus many enrichment areas.
For more GoodYearBooks, contact your local bookseller or educational dealer.
For a complete catalog with information about other GoodYearBooks, please
write:

GoodYearBooks

ScottForesman
1900 East Lake Avenue
Glenview, IL 60025

Book design by Amy O'Brien Krupp.

PREFACE

The purpose of *The Continents* is to inform students about the geographic, economic, and political nature of our world. We see this puzzle book as an aid to teachers who wish to help students learn more about our world through interesting and challenging classroom and homework assignments.

The World Book Encyclopedia is the factual information source for the puzzles found here, although identical facts are found in other reference materials. Our world is in a constant state of flux, therefore, countries change, new political figures arise daily, boundaries flex and bend, and transformation is the only constant. We have tried to create puzzles and games about the world's countries that will be current for a number of years. As we write this, however, the U.S.S.R. has become the Commonwealth of Independent States, and Yugoslavia is now a land of several countries. In addition, new spellings for particular place names seem to be introduced almost constantly. We have attempted to use spellings that are widely accepted for most items.

Change is our present and future way of life. Books cannot be immediately revised with each political upheaval or natural disaster, so children must be taught to go to current sources for their information and realize that some information sources are possibly out-of-date by the time books are printed.

Geographers and others who deal with labeling our world are not always in agreement as to what constitutes a continent. There is a general consensus that there are seven continents—Africa, Antarctica, Australia, Asia, Europe, North America, and South America. (We included New Zealand with Australia because of its importance.) Some consider Europe a peninsula of Asia and call the entire land mass Eurasia. We follow the more traditional view.

Each section of continents is preceded by a reproducible map of the continent with names of countries, cities, rivers, and other locations. The games, of course, are reproducible for classroom use, also.

Our hope is that many children will find the study of our world so fascinating through the medium of these puzzles and games that they will be caught up in a lifelong desire to learn more about the continents of this world.

Jeanne Cheyney
Arnold Cheyney

CONTENTS

From *The Continents*, published by GoodYearBooks. Copyright © 1994 Jeanne and Arnold Cheyney.

From *The Continents*, published by GoodYearBooks. Copyright © 1994 Jeanne and Arnold Cheyney.

THE
CONTINENTS
Puzzles for Learning World Geography

AFRICA

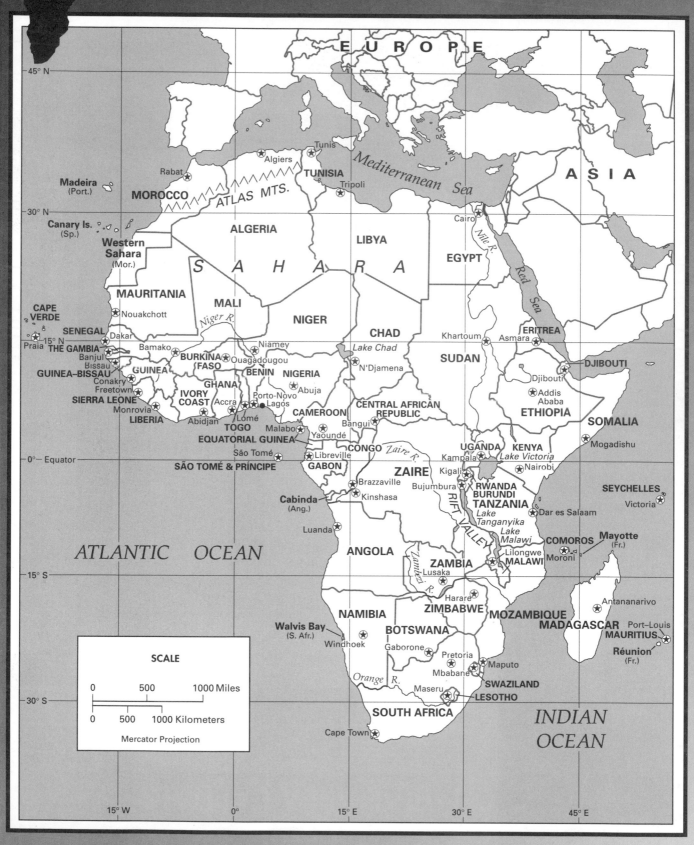

E U R O P E

45° N

ASIA

Mediterranean Sea

Tunis
Algiers
Rabat
TUNISIA
Tripoli
MOROCCO
ATLAS MTS.
30° N
Cairo
Madeira
(Port.)
Canary Is.
(Sp.)
ALGERIA
LIBYA
Nile R.
EGYPT
Western
Sahara
(Mor.)
S A H A R A
Red Sea
Khartoum
Asmara
ERITREA
MAURITANIA
MALI
Nouakchott
Niger R.
NIGER
CHAD
CAPE
VERDE
SENEGAL
Dakar
Bamako
Niamey
Lake Chad
SUDAN
DJIBOUTI
15° N
Praia
THE GAMBIA
Banjul
Bissau
BURKINA
FASO
Ouagadougou
N'Djamena
Djibouti
GUINEA-BISSAU
GUINEA
BENIN
NIGERIA
Addis
Ababa
Conakry
Freetown
GHANA
Abuja
CENTRAL AFRICAN
REPUBLIC
ETHIOPIA
SIERRA LEONE
IVORY
COAST
Accra
Porto-Novo
Lagos
SOMALIA
Monrovia
Abidjan
Lomé
TOGO
Malabo
Yaoundé
CAMEROON
Bangui
Mogadishu
LIBERIA
EQUATORIAL GUINEA
São Tomé
Libreville
Zaire R.
UGANDA
KENYA
Lake Victoria
0° Equator
SÃO TOMÉ & PRÍNCIPE
GABON
ZAIRE
Kampala
Nairobi
Kigali
SEYCHELLES
Cabinda
(Ang.)
Brazzaville
CONGO
Bujumbura
RWANDA
BURUNDI
Victoria
Kinshasa
TANZANIA
Dar es Salaam
Luanda
*Lake
Tanganyika*
RIFT VALLEY
*Lake
Malawi*
COMOROS
Mayotte
(Fr.)
Lilongwe
Moroni
MALAWI
15° S
ATLANTIC OCEAN
ANGOLA
ZAMBIA
Lusaka
Zambezi R.
Harare
Antananarivo
Walvis Bay
(S. Afr.)
NAMIBIA
ZIMBABWE
MOZAMBIQUE
MADAGASCAR
Port-Louis
MAURITIUS
Windhoek
BOTSWANA
Réunion
(Fr.)
Gaborone
Pretoria
Maputo
Orange R.
Mbabane
SWAZILAND
30° S
Maseru
LESOTHO
SOUTH AFRICA
INDIAN
OCEAN
Cape Town

SCALE

0   500   1000 Miles

0   500   1000 Kilometers

Mercator Projection

15° W   0°   15° E   30° E   45° E

From *The Continents*, published by GoodYearBooks. Copyright © 1994 Jeanne and Arnold Cheyney.

Name _____ Date _____

CROSSWORD PUZZLE

ACROSS

1. Nomads living in the Sahara Desert are called _____.
3. The world's longest river
4. South of the Sahara Desert, most people are _____ (color).
7. Many North-African rural homes are made of _____.
9. Valuable cash crop: _____ beans
12. Africa: the world's _____-largest continent area (about four times the size of the U.S. mainland)
17. Important wet-area food crop
18. Sahara Desert: almost as big as the _____
19. Western and Central Africa have _____ forests.
21. Much of Africa is covered with _____ land.
22. Eastern and southern grassland crop
23. Important meats for food: lamb, _____, goat

DOWN

2. Africa: the world's largest producer of _____ (a valuable gem stone)
4. A North-African open-air market is called a _____.
5. A wild grassland animal
6. In Northern Africa, most of the people are _____ (have Arabian ancestry).
8. An important basic food: flat _____
10. Chores of rural African women: carry water, collect firewood, grind _____
11. Africa's highest volcanic peak
13. (Africa, south of the Sahara Desert): about 75 percent of the people live in _____ areas.
14. Africa has 52 independent _____.
15. Sahara Desert nomads raise _____, goats, and sheep.
16. The world's largest desert is the _____.
19. A wet area food crop
20. (1400s & 1500s) The Europeans had a gold trade and a _____ trade in Africa.

Acacia Tree

Name _____ Date _____

CROSSWORD PUZZLE

ACROSS

2. Country south of Senegal; northwest of Guinea: Guinea-_____

4. Country southwest of Mali; north of Sierra Leone

6. Country west of Chad; east of Mali

10. Country west of Mali; north of Senegal

15. Country between Niger and Sudan

16. Country southwest of Mali; southwest of Mauritania

DOWN

1. Country east of Sudan

2. Country south of Mali: _____ Faso

3. Country east of Morocco; west of Libya

5. Country east of Mauritania; north of Burkina Faso

7. Country northwest of Algeria; on the North Atlantic Ocean

8. Country surrounded by Senegal; on the North Atlantic Ocean

9. Country between Algeria and Egypt

11. Country on the Mediterranean Sea; northwest of Libya

12. Country east of Libya; north of Sudan

13. Country south of Egypt; east of Chad

14. Island country west of Dakar, Senegal, in the Atlantic Ocean: Cape_____

Rural Northern Village

^ ^

Name _____   Date _____

CROSSWORD PUZZLE

Palm Trees

ACROSS
1. Capital of Chad
3. Capital of Gambia
5. Capital of Tunisia
7. Capital of Burkina Faso
9. Capital of Mali
10. Capital of Sudan
11. Capital of Morocco
15. Capital of Libya
17. Capital of Guinea-Bissau

DOWN
2. Capital of Senegal
4. Capital of Guinea
6. Capital of Mauritania
8. Capital of Cape Verde
12. Capital of Ethiopia: _____ Ababa
13. Capital of Niger
14. Capital of Algeria
16. Capital of Egypt

A Capital

From *The Continents*, published by GoodYearBooks. Copyright © 1994 Jeanne and Arnold Cheyney.

Name _____ Date _____

CROSSWORD PUZZLE

Bamboo Hut

ACROSS

2. Country south of Chad; southwest of Sudan: Central _____ Republic
5. Country west of Kenya; south of Sudan
6. Country west of Zaire; east of Gabon
11. Country east of Ethiopia; northwest of Somalia

Dugout Canoe

12. Country west of Ghana; east of Liberia: _____ Coast
15. Country east of Ivory Coast; west of Togo
16. Country south of Guinea; northwest of Liberia: Sierra _____
17. Country west of Congo; south of Cameroon

DOWN

1. Country between Togo and Nigeria
3. Country east of Nigeria; west of Central African Republic
4. Country east of Ethiopia; on the Indian Ocean
7. Country south of Niger; west of Cameroon
8. Country north of Sierra Leone; southwest of Mali
9. Country east of Sierra Leone; west of Ivory Coast
10. Country east of Ghana; west of Benin
13. Island country in the Gulf of Guinea; west of Gabon: São _____ and Príncipe
14. Country bordering the Indian Ocean; south of Ethiopia

From *The Continents*, published by GoodYearBooks. Copyright © 1994 Jeanne and Arnold Cheyney.

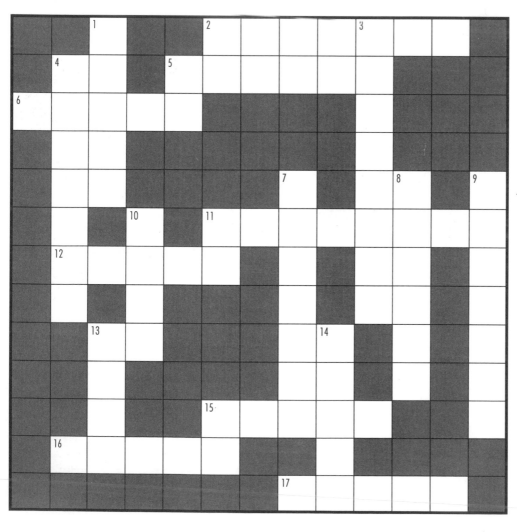

Outdoor Market

Name _____ Date _____

CROSSWORD PUZZLE

ACROSS

1. Capital of Djibouti
3. Capital of São Tomé and Príncipe: _____ Tomé
5. Capital of Sierra Leone
6. Former capital of Nigeria
9. Capital of Benin: _____-Novo
12. Capital of Ivory Coast
15. Capital of Kenya
16. Capital of Gabon
17. Capital of Togo

DOWN

2. Capital of Congo
4. Capital of Ghana
7. Capital of Somalia
8. Capital of Uganda
10. Capital of Central African Republic
11. Capital of Equatorial Guinea
13. Capital of Liberia
14. Capital of Cameroon

A Central-Area Capital Scene

Name _____ Date _____

CROSSWORD PUZZLE

ACROSS

2. An island country east of Madagascar; in the Indian Ocean
3. Country east of Namibia; north of South Africa
4. Country east of Angola; south of Zaire
6. Country nearly surrounded by South Africa; south of Mozambique
7. Country east of Zambia; extending into north-central Mozambique
9. Country north of Namibia; west of Zambia
16. A very large island east of Mozambique; south of Comoros Islands
17. Country north of Zambia; west of Tanzania

DOWN

1. Country of islands in the Indian Ocean; east of Tanzania
2. Country west of Madagascar; east of Zimbabwe
5. Country west of Mozambique; south of Zambia
8. Country of islands east of Mozambique; north-west of Madagascar
10. Country south of Angola; west of Botswana
11. Country east of Zaire; northwest of Tanzania
12. Country east of Zaire; southwest of Kenya
13. Country north of Burundi; southwest of Uganda
14. Small country entirely within South Africa
15. Country south of Botswana; south of Namibia: South _____

Village

From *The Continents*, published by GoodYearBooks. Copyright © 1994 Jeanne and Arnold Cheyney.

SOUTHERN-AREA CAPITALS AFRICA

Name _____   Date _____

CROSSWORD PUZZLE

ACROSS

1. Capital of Mozambique
4. Capital of Burundi
5. Capital of Namibia
9. Capital of Tanzania: _____ es Salaam
13. Capital of Madagascar
15. Capital of Mauritius: Port _____
16. Capital of Rwanda
17. Capital of Seychelles

DOWN

1. Capital of Lesotho
2. Capital of Angola
3. Legislative Capital of South Africa: _____ Town
6. Capital of Swaziland
7. Capital of Zimbabwe
8. Capital of Botswana
10. Capital of Zaire
11. Capital of Comoros
12. Capital of Malawi
14. Capital of Zambia

Market

Name _____   Date _____

CROSSWORD PUZZLE

ACROSS

1. On the Plateaus: in the rainy season, small salty lakes called _____ appear
8. Four-fifths of Algeria is part of the _____ Desert.
10. Capital and largest city
14. Rich deposits of _____ are under the sandy desert.
15. Most farmers raise cattle, sheep, and _____, or farm a little land.
18. Most favorite sport
19. A fruit crop
20. The Tell: coastal area that includes good _____ land
25. The first-known people to live in Algeria

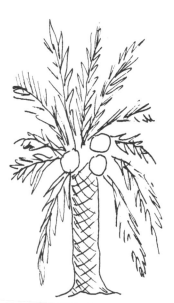

Date Palm

DOWN

2. Highest mountain peak
3. A favorite national dish (food)
4. Women's white outer garment
5. Algeria is located in _____ Africa
6. A crop
7. A chief farm crop
9. A fruit crop
11. Men's long hooded cloak
12. A dairy product
13. Many rural homes are built of _____ and straw or stone.
16. _____ (country) once ruled Algeria
17. A chief farm crop
21. A house of worship
22. Most people live in _____ (place).
23. A special tree: _____ oak
24. The coastal area is called the _____ and has good farmland.

From *The Continents*, published by GoodYearBooks. Copyright © 1994 Jeanne and Arnold Cheyney.

Name _____ Date _____

NAME THE CITY
DIRECTIONS

Fill in the dotted lines with your answers. If they are correct, the circled letters will spell the name of Congo's largest city.

1. A tropical fruit crop

2. Most valuable mineral and export

3. People in the thick forest of northern Congo travel by dugout _____.

4. Country east of Congo

5. Congo's capital

6. Congo borders the South _____ Ocean.

7. The Niari _____ has good farmland.

8. Congo is hot and _____.

9. A chief forest export

10. A chief crop: palm _____

11. Imaginary line running through Congo

1. ◯ __ __ __ __

2. __ __ __ ◯ __ __ __ __

3. __ ◯ __ __ __ __

4. ◯ __ __ __ __

5. __ __ __ ◯ __ __ __ __ __

6. ◯ __ __ __ __ __ __

7. __ __ ◯ __ __ __ __

8. __ __ __ ◯ __

9. ◯ __ __ __ __

10. __ __ ◯ __

11. ◯ __ __ __ __ __ __

CONGO CLUE
DIRECTIONS

Each set of lines has a vowel to help you determine the correct answer. All the words tell about Congo.

Some chief crops:

__ e __ __ __ __ __

__ __ __ e __ __ __ __

__ __ __ __ e __

__ __ __ __ __ __ __ __ e

Chief river:

__ o __ __ o

Northern Congo has thick:

__ o __ __ __ __ __

Official language:

__ __ e __ __ __

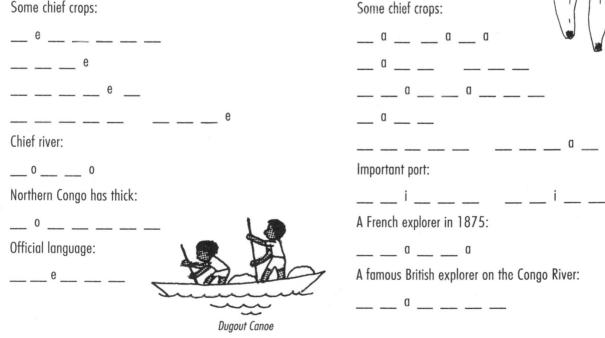

Dugout Canoe

Some chief crops:

__ a __ __ a __ a

__ a __ __ __ __ __ __

__ __ a __ __ a __ __ __

__ a __ __

__ __ __ __ __ __ __ __ a __ __ __ __

Important port:

__ __ i __ __ __ __ __ i __ __

A French explorer in 1875:

__ __ __ a __ __ a

A famous British explorer on the Congo River:

__ __ __ a __ __ __

Bananas

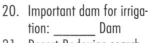

Name _____ Date _____

CROSSWORD PUZZLE

ACROSS

1. Kings, called _____, were buried in the pyramids.
3. A western border country
9. The _____ Sea borders northern Egypt.
11. A huge, famous statue with the body of a lion and head of a man: The Great _____
13. Crops must be _____ to survive.
14. Desert Bedouins ride on _____ and sleep in tents.
16. Most of the people live along the Nile River and _____ Canal.
17. Approximately one/half of the people live in rural areas and are _____ peasants called fellahin.
19. South border country
22. Chief seaport
23. Nearly all of Egypt is part of the _____ Desert.
24. Bedouin men wrap their heads with cloth to keep out sand and _____.
25. Egyptians eat mostly _____.

DOWN

1. Tourists come to see the _____ (burial places of ancient kings).
2. Egyptians developed the first _____ (using 365 days).
4. Most important field crop
5. Almost all of the _____ land is along the Nile River.

6. Eastern border: Gulf of Suez and the _____ Sea
7. The capital, _____, is the largest city in Africa and the Arab world.
8. Chief liquid mineral export
10. The _____ River gives Egypt most of its water.

12. An important crop: _____ cane
15. God gave _____ the Ten Commandments on Mount Sinai.
18. Egypt: the world's largest producer of _____ (a fruit)

20. Important dam for irrigation: _____ Dam
21. Desert Bedouins search for pastures for their _____, camels, and sheep.

Pyramids

From *The Continents*, published by GoodYearBooks. Copyright © 1994 Jeanne and Arnold Cheyney.

Name _____ Date _____

D	E	R	Q	M	K	S	T	C	F	S	Y	N
A	C	O	R	A	B	I	F	O	D	F	K	P
A	B	Y	S	S	I	N	I	A	L	B	E	J
H	G	A	E	O	F	N	E	S	K	P	Y	T
O	N	D	J	C	N	E	S	T	U	H	E	I
W	I	C	I	C	I	T	H	T	A	Q	K	H
H	C	A	M	E	L	S	A	R	U	W	N	C
E	Z	T	N	R	E	R	M	S	T	A	O	G
A	F	T	P	S	A	O	M	O	V	F	M	S
T	O	L	M	G	W	M	A	P	F	S	G	N
C	H	E	U	E	S	T	S	E	R	O	F	E
F	O	S	S	I	L	S	E	E	W	X	W	K
S	Y	R	A	X	V	D	M	H	I	A	G	C
E	J	D	N	W	T	R	H	S	B	N	A	I
C	C	G	I	R	A	F	F	E	C	O	Y	H
A	R	L	B	F	N	S	T	U	K	I	Z	C
F	Q	E	L	L	A	B	Y	E	L	L	O	V

farmers (Most Ethiopians are)
(Favorite sports:)
    soccer
    tennis
    volleyball
(In Greek, Ethiopia means
    sunburned) faces
(Most farmers have:)
    cattle
    chickens
    goats
    sheep
Omo (River)
Red (Sea: the northern
    border)
(Red Sea) coast (one of the
    world's hottest places)
(round) huts (most people live
    in them)
shammas (one-piece cotton
    cloths worn by men and
    women)
(Some of world's oldest
    human) fossils (found)
Tana (largest lake)
(tropical rain) forests
Wabe (Shebele River)
wat (stew of meat,
    vegetables, eggs)
(Wild animals:)
    giraffe
    lion
    monkey

WORD SEARCHING

DIRECTIONS

The grid above contains hidden words. They can go up, down, across, at an angle, forward, or backward. The hidden words appear in bold print in the list to the right.

Abyssinia (Ethiopia's former
    name)
Awash (River)
Baro (River)
(Blue) Nile (River)
camels (to carry supplies)

(Chief crops:)
    corn
    sugar (cane)
    teff (grain)
    wheat
(Chief exports:)
    coffee
    hides

Dromedary

Name _____ Date _____

CROSSWORD PUZZLE

ACROSS

2. Coastal area: hot and humid, with beautiful sandy _____
5. A chief river
6. Most rural people have houses of _____ with thatched roofs.
7. A coastal area nut tree
8. A chief export
9. Many _____ visit Kenya to see the coastal area and animals.
12. A large bird
14. A striped wild animal
18. Highest mountain: Mount _____
20. Chief cash crop
21. Kenya nomads: _____ (tall, slim people skilled in weapons use)
22. Chief port
23. Most popular sports: _____ plus track and field
24. An abbreviated word for a large wild animal
25. Capital and largest city
26. A farm crop: _____ potato

DOWN

1. People who hunt illegally and help cause animals to be extinct
3. Imaginary line running through the center of Kenya
4. The people are nearly all _____ (color) Africans.
10. Kenya borders the _____ Ocean.
11. Most people are _____ (occupation) and raise livestock.
13. A favorite recreation
15. The best _____ land: southwest mountains and plateaus
16. Movies are taken by mobile units to _____ areas.
17. Part of Kenya's western border: Lake _____ (Africa's largest lake)
19. The basic food is corn called _____.

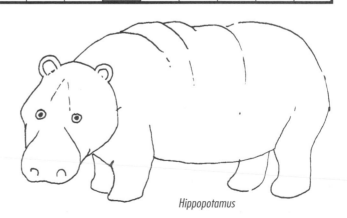

Hippopotamus

14 ^

From *The Continents*, published by GoodYearBooks. Copyright © 1994 Jeanne and Arnold Cheyney.

Name _____   Date _____

CROSSWORD PUZZLE

ACROSS

1. One of the world's largest shipping fleets: other world countries register their _____ under the Liberian flag to save tax money on shipping.

4. Location: on the _____ Ocean; west of Ivory Coast

6. _____ forests cover much of the country.

9. Liberia: formerly named Monrovia in honor of U.S. President James _____ (1812)

13. January: a cool, dry wind that blows red dust toward the coast

18. Chief cash crop

21. Only people with black _____ can become citizens.

22. A chief crop

DOWN

1. Liberia: founded in 1822, by an American group, to give a home to U.S. freed _____ and to slaves on ships sailing toward the U.S.

2. Important vegetable crop

3. Most rural people are _____ (occupation).

5. Liberia has one of the world's richest _____ ore deposits.

7. Official language

8. _____: long cloth wrapped around the waist for a skirt

10. Most farmers raise _____ and chickens.

11. Capital and largest city

12. People in cities go to the _____ (four initials—for exercise, just like Americans).

14. Popular sports: _____ and soccer

15. Some rural people work on _____ ships or fish (occupations).

16. Climate: hot and _____

17. An important forest export

18. A chief crop

19. A wild animal that destroys crops

20. People in cities go to see _____ (entertainment).

Goat

^ ^

Name _____ Date _____

NAME THE PIRATE WHO SAILED TO MADAGASCAR

DIRECTIONS

Fill in the dotted lines with your answers. If they are correct, the circled letters will spell the name of a daring pirate.

1. Most valuable export

2. World's chief producer of this flavoring

3. A vegetable crop

4. Most important livestock

5. Capital and largest city

6. Reefs and storms make the east coast dangerous for _____.

7. A country that once ruled Madagascar

8. Streets in the capital are crowded on _____ day.

9. Chief food crop

10. Chief occupations of most people are farmers and _____.

11. A farm animal product export

1. ○ _ _ _ _

2. _ ○ _ _ _ _ _

3. _ _ _ _ ○ _ _ _ _

4. _ _ ○ _ _ _

5. _ _ _ _ _ _ _ _ _ _ _ _

6. _ _ ○ _ _

7. _ _ _ ○ _ _

8. _ _ _ ○ _ _ _

9. _ _ ○ _ _ _

10. _ _ _ ○ _ _ _

11. _ _ ○ _ _

MADAGASCAR SCRAMBLED WORDS

DIRECTIONS

Unscramble the words and write the answers on the lines provided. (Use scrap paper to work out your answers.)

1. Wild animal found only on Madagascar and Comoros

   u e l r m   _____

2. World's leading producer of this spice

   v l s c o e   _____

3. Largest group of people on Madagascar are from this continent

   r a a c f i   _____

4. Second largest group of people on Madagascar are from this country

   a d e i i n o n s   _____

5. Madagascar is east of what African country?

   q b o i e z m m a u   _____

Lemur

^ ^

From *The Continents*, published by GoodYearBooks. Copyright © 1994 Jeanne and Arnold Cheyney.

Name _____ Date _____

SUPPLY THE VOWEL

DIRECTIONS

This grid contains hidden words. The hidden words appear in bold print in the list below. The words can go up, down, across, at angles, backward, or forward. Parts of words may overlap. Supply the correct vowel—
a e i o u—for the center of each word group.

(carved) **masks** (made by rain-forest people)

(Great) **Britain** (once ruled Nigeria)

(Important crops:)
corn
beans
rice
yams

(Important farm animals:)
cattle
goats
sheep

Lagos (former capital and largest city)

(A leading world producer of:)
(palm) **oil**
peanuts
rubber

movies (popular city entertainment)

mud (used to build homes)

Niger (River, with big delta)

petroleum (valuable mineral supplying wealth)

Shebshi (Mountains)

shrimp (coastal catch)

soccer (most popular sport)

A	D	T	O	S	K	B	C	O	D	M	R	Z
N	F	V	K	B	Z	P	E	A	N	◯	T	S
C	Y	S	J	Y	S	C	K	F	B	E	M	E
L	◯	G	O	S	I	N	C	B	D	L	L	B
M	M	T	D	A	G	P	E	W	H	O	X	M
I	S	K	T	A	V	R	U	K	Y	R	E	U
T	H	S	Y	L	R	R	M	S	C	T	R	E
S	R	N	D	I	E	B	L	H	N	E	M	W
J	H	A	C	P	Q	K	R	R	G	P	L	Z
S	H	◯	E	P	R	O	L	◯	O	N	Q	U
R	W	B	B	E	C	B	N	M	T	C	G	P
U	E	V	T	S	T	F	W	P	S	A	C	B
J	P	C	A	T	H	U	M	H	V	Y	I	J
L	N	S	C	A	C	I	E	L	G	P	E	N
D	I	X	M	◯	V	I	E	S	I	H	O	F
G	Y	H	R	G	S	B	M	A	Q	D	B	R
R	S	N	G	F	S	J	I	T	O	F	W	A

Herders

From *The Continents*, published by GoodYearBooks. Copyright © 1994 Jeanne and Arnold Cheyney.

Name _____ Date _____

CROSSWORD PUZZLE

ACROSS

4. Wild animals in _____ National Park are a tourist attraction.
7. A policy of racial segregation is called _____ .
8. A poultry product
9. A farm crop
11. Chief farm-product export
12. A leading fruit crop
13. South Africa: most highly developed and _____ country of Africa
18. Many non-whites have low-_____ jobs.
23. South of the equator: seasons are _____ from the Northern Hemisphere

10. South Africa's longest river: _____ River
14. Whites from _____, Scotland, and Ireland are business people.
15. A world leader in raising _____
16. Blacks are mostly _____, miners, and laborers.

17. A wild animal in the National Park
19. _____ people control the government, but there are few of them.
20. Very dry area: _____ Desert
21. Many Asians (mostly Indians) sell vegetables or _____ in factories.

22. Farmers produce nearly all the needed _____ .

Sheep

DOWN

1. Most of the people are _____ Africans.
2. Most whites, whose ancestors were usually from the Netherlands, Germany, or France, are called _____ .
3. South Africa: approximately _____ times as large as California
5. Johannesburg area: world's richest _____ field
6. The government divides South Africa into four _____ groups: Whites, Coloreds, Asians, Blacks.
9. Three capitals: _____ Town, Pretoria, and Bloemfontein

Name _____ Date _____

NUMBER CODE

A - 1	G - 7	M - 13	S - 19	Y - 25
B - 2	H - 8	N - 14	T - 20	Z - 26
C - 3	I - 9	O - 15	U - 21	
D - 4	J - 10	P - 16	V - 22	
E - 5	K - 11	Q - 17	W - 23	
F - 6	L - 12	R - 18	X - 24	

DIRECTIONS

Look at the number under each line. Find the matching number in the code box. Write the letter that matches that number on the answer lines below.

1. What is the largest African lake that forms part of Uganda's boundary?

‾22‾ ‾9‾ ‾3‾ ‾20‾ ‾15‾ ‾18‾ ‾9‾ ‾1‾   ‾12‾ ‾1‾ ‾11‾ ‾5‾

2. What is the capital and largest city?

‾11‾ ‾1‾ ‾13‾ ‾16‾ ‾1‾ ‾12‾ ‾1‾

Cotton

3. What do most of the people do for a living, and who does much of the labor?

‾6‾ ‾1‾ ‾18‾ ‾13‾'   ‾1‾ ‾14‾ ‾4‾   ‾23‾ ‾15‾ ‾13‾ ‾5‾ ‾14‾   ‾4‾ ‾15‾   ‾1‾

‾12‾ ‾15‾ ‾20‾   ‾15‾ ‾6‾   ‾20‾ ‾8‾ ‾5‾   ‾23‾ ‾15‾ ‾18‾ ‾11‾

4. What is a savanna?

‾7‾ ‾18‾ ‾1‾ ‾19‾ ‾19‾ ‾12‾ ‾1‾ ‾14‾ ‾4‾   ‾23‾ ‾9‾ ‾20‾ ‾8‾   ‾12‾ ‾15‾ ‾23‾

‾20‾ ‾18‾ ‾5‾ ‾5‾ ‾19‾

5. This describes Uganda.

‾8‾ ‾9‾ ‾7‾ ‾8‾   ‾16‾ ‾12‾ ‾1‾ ‾20‾ ‾5‾ ‾1‾ ‾21‾   ‾1‾ ‾14‾ ‾4‾   ‾13‾ ‾9‾ ‾12‾ ‾4‾

‾20‾ ‾5‾ ‾13‾ ‾16‾ ‾5‾ ‾18‾ ‾1‾ ‾20‾ ‾21‾ ‾18‾ ‾5‾ ‾19‾

6. What are the chief crops?

‾2‾ ‾1‾ ‾14‾ ‾1‾ ‾14‾ ‾1‾ ‾19‾,   ‾2‾ ‾5‾ ‾1‾ ‾14‾ ‾19‾,   ‾3‾ ‾1‾ ‾19‾ ‾19‾ ‾1‾ ‾22‾ ‾1‾,

‾3‾ ‾15‾ ‾18‾ ‾14‾,   ‾13‾ ‾9‾ ‾12‾ ‾12‾ ‾5‾ ‾20‾,   ‾19‾ ‾23‾ ‾5‾ ‾5‾ ‾20‾

‾16‾ ‾15‾ ‾20‾ ‾1‾ ‾20‾ ‾15‾ ‾5‾ ‾19‾

7. What are the exports?

‾3‾ ‾15‾ ‾6‾ ‾6‾ ‾5‾ ‾5‾,   ‾3‾ ‾15‾ ‾20‾ ‾20‾ ‾15‾ ‾14‾,   ‾19‾ ‾21‾ ‾7‾ ‾1‾ ‾18‾

‾3‾ ‾1‾ ‾14‾ ‾5‾;   ‾20‾ ‾5‾ ‾1‾   ‾9‾ ‾19‾   ‾13‾ ‾15‾ ‾19‾ ‾20‾

‾9‾ ‾13‾ ‾16‾ ‾15‾ ‾18‾ ‾20‾ ‾1‾ ‾14‾ ‾20‾

Picking Tea

19. Basic foods for most people: corn, _____, cassava (manioc meal, w/sauce)
21. Best-known art: carved wooden statues and _____
23. Capital and largest city
24. The farm people are _____.
25. Rural people enjoy tribal _____ accompanied by drum music.
26. A rain-forest product: _____ oil

DOWN

2. A crop grown on small farms
4. A chief river for transportation
9. The rain forest is so thick that _____ seldom gets through it.
10. A rain-forest product
11. Men set traps in the Congo R. for _____.
12. A rain forest product
13. Large, long eastern lake
14. A world leader in mining _____ and industrial diamonds
16. The government wants no _____ influence and discourages wearing western-style clothes.
17. A wild animal (cat family) with heavy mane on male
18. A spotted wild animal (cat family)
20. Zaire: one of the world's largest _____ forests, covering 1/3 of the country
22. Most of the people _____ some land.

Lion

CROSSWORD PUZZLE

ACROSS

1. Nearly all the people are _____ (color).
3. A large reptile that lives in water
5. A wild mammal related to the horse
6. Many people suffer from _____ (lack of necessary nutrients).
7. Black people of very small size (in Zaire)
8. Favorite spectator sport
15. _____ (country) once ruled Zaire.

From *The Continents*, published by GoodYearBooks. Copyright © 1994 Jeanne and Arnold Cheyney.

^ ^

Name _____ Date _____

SAHARA DESERT CLUE

DIRECTIONS

Each set of lines has a vowel to help you determine the correct answer. All the words tell about the Sahara Desert.

Oasis crops:

__ a __ __ __

__ a __ __ __ __

__ __ __ a __

Desert animals:

__ e __ __ __ __ __

__ __ __ __ e __

__ __ e e __

__ __ __ e __ __ e __

Occasionally seen on mountain peaks:

__ __ o __

Rain:

some areas, less than one i __ __ __ per year.

Nights are:

__ o o __

Sometimes, 600 feet high:

__ u __ __ __

Some plants only last six or eight __ e e __ __

Once crossed the desert on trading routes:

__ a __ a __ a __ __

In ancient times, there were __ a __ __ __ and people

__ i __ __ __ __.

SAHARA DESERT SKYSCRAPER

DIRECTIONS

Write your answers in the boxes. The circled letters will help you.

1. Sahara Desert: about the size of the _____

2. Under the sand, in some areas, are great deposits of

   _____.

3. Great seas of sand are called _____.

4. About ninety fertile areas where crops grow and people live:

   _____

5. Chief desert transportation

6. The Sahara: the world's _____ desert

7. The Sahara: extends from the Red Sea to the _____ Ocean

8. The Sahara Desert has some _____.

9. The Sahara covers most of the country of _____.

10. Oases have _____ water.

Gerboa

1.
2.
3.
4.
5. Ⓔ
6. Ⓡ
7.
8. Ⓜ
9. Ⓘ
10. Ⓓ

From *The Continents*, published by GoodYearBooks. Copyright © 1994 Jeanne and Arnold Cheyney.

^ ^

AFRICA TREES AND PLANTS

Name _____ Date _____

WORD SEARCHING

DIRECTIONS

This grid contains hidden words. The hidden words appear in bold print in the list below. They can go up, down, across, at an angle, forward, or backward.

Acacia (tree)

(African) **Mahogany** (tree)

(African) **Tulip** (tree)

Aloe (plant)

(Atlas) **Cedar** (tree)

Bamboo (plant)

Banana (plant)

Baobab (tree)

Cacao (tree)

Coffee (plant)

Cork (oak, tree)

Date (palm, tree)

Ebony (tree)

Elephant (grass, plant)

Incense (tree)

Kapok (tree)

Kola (nut tree)

Mangrove (tree)

Mimosa (tree)

Myrrh (plant)

(Oil) **Palm** (tree)

Okoumé (tree)

Olive (tree)

Papaya (tree)

Papyrus (plant)

Shea (Nut tree)

(Yellow) **Satinwood** (tree)

A	I	C	A	C	A	S	B	E	A	L	P	C
B	N	V	S	O	A	M	H	V	S	A	I	A
M	C	R	M	F	G	C	N	I	T	P	L	S
Y	E	E	G	F	D	R	A	L	Y	I	U	E
B	N	M	N	E	O	K	R	O	C	R	T	C
A	S	U	B	E	T	A	D	M	Y	R	R	H
T	E	O	F	P	W	S	C	P	M	W	O	S
B	N	K	U	P	A	P	A	Y	A	D	E	A
Y	A	O	L	A	N	P	R	H	N	T	D	T
M	L	B	Y	L	A	E	H	S	G	E	Y	I
A	F	U	O	M	N	X	C	J	R	O	N	N
H	M	K	W	A	A	I	O	K	O	L	A	W
O	O	B	M	A	B	D	K	N	V	A	G	O
G	E	K	U	P	L	R	A	D	E	C	O	O
A	M	I	M	O	S	A	Y	J	F	Q	H	D
N	G	K	B	H	E	U	I	K	A	P	O	K
Y	T	Z	T	N	A	H	P	E	L	E	M	J

Cork Oak

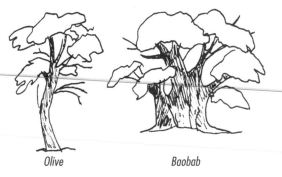

Olive   *Baobab*

From *The Continents*, published by GoodYearBooks. Copyright © 1994 Jeanne and Arnold Cheyney.

Name _____ Date _____

CROSSING OVER

DIRECTIONS

Use a pencil for this game. Find words from the following list (the words not in parentheses) that have the correct number of spaces and letters to fit into the crossing-over boxes. Each word has a place where it belongs. The first word is done for you. To continue, find a 9-letter word with "p" in the sixth space and so on. All the words tell about wild animals in Africa.

3 letters
(Barbary) ape
gnu
(wart) hog

4 letters
(Cape) seal
ibis
lion

5 letters
eland
hyena
(Mamba) snake
okapi
zebra

6 letters
aoudad
baboon
Dorcas (gazelle)
fennec
(Guereza) monkey
impala
jackal
jerboa
(Rock) python
serval

7 letters
(Cape) buffalo
cheetah
(Dama) gazelle
giraffe
gorilla
(Jackass) penguin
leopard

ostrich
vulture

8 letters
aardvark
antelope
elephant
flamingo

9 letters
crocodile
dromedary (camel)
porcupine

10 letters
chimpanzee
rhinoceros

12 letters
hippopotamus

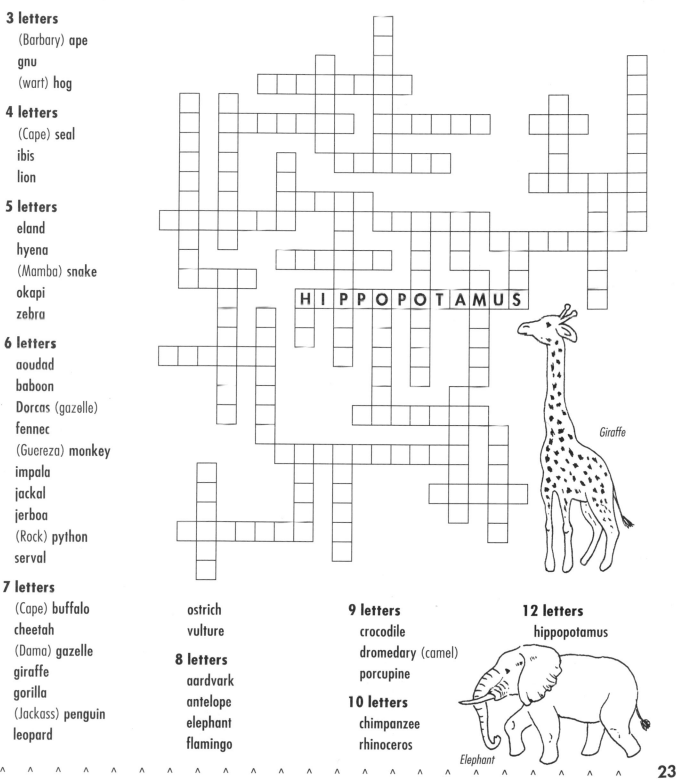

HIPPOPOTAMUS

Giraffe

Elephant

Name _____ Date _____

SUPPLY THE VOWEL

DIRECTIONS

This grid contains hidden words. The hidden words appear in bold print in the list at the right. The words can go up, down, across, at angles, backward, or forward. Parts of words may overlap. Supply the correct vowel—a e i o u—for the center of each word group.

bauxite (for making aluminum)

cacao (for cocoa and chocolate)

cashews (nuts)

citrus (fruit)

cloves (spice)

coffee

copra (dried coconut meat)

cotton

dates

diamonds

hides

iron

peanuts

petroleum

rubber

shrimp

sisal (for rope)

skins

tea

timber

A	C	E	K	D	S	P	M	Y	S	L	H	P
D	G	L	O	I	E	N	H	T	W	R	O	Y
C	O	P	R	◯	B	V	D	S	◯	T	A	D
R	A	T	N	M	C	E	U	B	H	A	B	H
W	F	U	D	O	L	A	M	P	S	R	N	M
R	T	O	E	N	Q	I	C	R	A	L	W	Q
S	E	C	S	D	T	E	D	S	C	A	F	T
C	F	B	R	S	P	B	A	I	N	S	H	B
I	J	N	B	M	S	K	S	H	R	◯	M	P
E	T	I	X	◯	A	B	L	U	D	S	K	M
F	N	S	R	E	R	I	O	E	G	D	F	S
O	I	T	K	L	E	U	S	S	P	K	W	I
B	I	J	M	O	S	F	Y	E	T	B	R	S
C	A	C	U	R	M	B	F	V	N	G	K	E
V	T	R	H	T	P	T	C	◯	T	T	O	N
J	N	E	W	E	C	O	R	L	C	J	Y	H
A	L	U	D	P	G	I	J	C	A	V	C	G

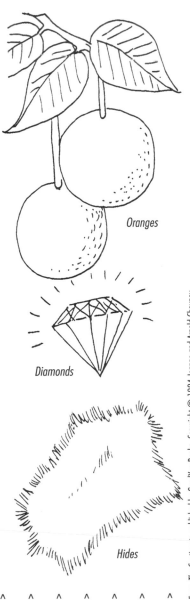

Oranges

Diamonds

Hides

^ ^

Name _____   Date _____

CROSSING OVER

DIRECTIONS

Use a pencil for this game. Find words from the following list (the words not in parentheses) that have the correct number of spaces and letters to fit into the crossing-over boxes. Each word has a place where it belongs. The first word is done for you. To continue, find a 6-letter word with "o" in the third space. All the words tell about chief farm products in Africa.

3 letters
tea

4 letters
corn
kola (nuts for soft drinks)
palm (oil)
rice
taro (edible underground stem)
wool (sheep)
yams

5 letters
cacao (for cocoa and chocolate)
copra (dried coconut meat)
dates
hides
sisal (for rope)
skins
sugar (cane)
sweet (potatoes)

6 letters
barley
cloves (spice)
coffee
cotton
ginger (spice)
millet
olives
rubber
sesame

7 letters
bananas
cashews
cassava (root crop)
oranges
(palm) kernels
peanuts
sorghum

8 letters
cinnamon
coconuts
piassava (for brushes, brooms, and mats)
plantain (banana-like food)

9 letters
pineapple

10 letters
watermelon

Pineapple

C O F F E E

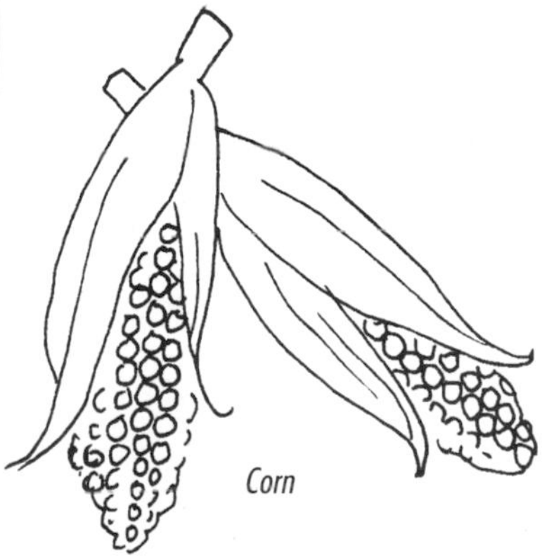

Corn

Olives

25

Name _____ Date _____

NUMBER CODE
BENIN THROUGH GAMBIA
DIRECTIONS

Look at the number under each line. Find the matching number in the code box. Write the letter that matches that number on the corresponding answer lines.

A - 1	G - 7	M - 13	S - 19	Y - 25
B - 2	H - 8	N - 14	T - 20	Z - 26
C - 3	I - 9	O - 15	U - 21	
D - 4	J - 10	P - 16	V - 22	
E - 5	K - 11	Q - 17	W - 23	
F - 6	L - 12	R - 18	X - 24	

1. Benin's lagoon area (inland from the coast):

   ‾2‾ ‾1‾ ‾13‾ ‾2‾ ‾15‾ ‾15‾   ‾8‾ ‾21‾ ‾20‾ ‾19‾   ‾2‾ ‾21‾ ‾9‾ ‾12‾ ‾20‾   ‾15‾ ‾14‾

   ‾19‾ ‾20‾ ‾1‾ ‾11‾ ‾5‾ ‾19‾   ‾1‾ ‾2‾ ‾15‾ ‾22‾ ‾5‾   ‾20‾ ‾8‾ ‾5‾   ‾23‾ ‾1‾ ‾20‾ ‾5‾ ‾18‾

2. Botswana: about 10,000 ‾2‾ ‾21‾ ‾19‾ ‾8‾ ‾13‾ ‾5‾ ‾14‾, ‾23‾ ‾9‾ ‾20‾ ‾8‾

   ‾25‾ ‾5‾ ‾12‾ ‾12‾ ‾15‾ ‾23‾ - ‾2‾ ‾18‾ ‾15‾ ‾23‾ ‾14‾   ‾19‾ ‾11‾ ‾9‾ ‾14‾,

   ‾19‾ ‾20‾ ‾9‾ ‾12‾ ‾12‾   ‾8‾ ‾21‾ ‾14‾ ‾20‾   ‾23‾ ‾9‾ ‾20‾ ‾8‾   ‾2‾ ‾15‾ ‾23‾ ‾19‾

   ‾1‾ ‾14‾ ‾4‾   ‾1‾ ‾18‾ ‾18‾ ‾15‾ ‾23‾ ‾19‾.

3. Burundi: ‾19‾ ‾15‾ ‾13‾ ‾5‾   ‾16‾ ‾5‾ ‾15‾ ‾16‾ ‾12‾ ‾5‾   ‾1‾ ‾18‾ ‾5‾

   ‾16‾ ‾25‾ ‾7‾ ‾13‾ ‾9‾ ‾5‾ ‾19‾   (‾19‾ ‾13‾ ‾1‾ ‾12‾ ‾12‾   ‾16‾ ‾5‾ ‾15‾ ‾16‾ ‾12‾ ‾5‾).

4. Cameroon's artists: ‾6‾ ‾1‾ ‾13‾ ‾15‾ ‾21‾ ‾19‾   ‾6‾ ‾15‾ ‾18‾   ‾13‾ ‾1‾ ‾19‾ ‾11‾

   ‾1‾ ‾14‾ ‾4‾   ‾19‾ ‾20‾ ‾1‾ ‾20‾ ‾21‾ ‾5‾ - ‾13‾ ‾1‾ ‾11‾ ‾9‾ ‾14‾ ‾7‾.

   Masks and Statues

5. Central African Republic has a dangerous pest:

   ‾20‾ ‾19‾ ‾5‾ ‾20‾ ‾19‾ ‾5‾   ‾6‾ ‾12‾ ‾25‾ - ‾3‾ ‾1‾ ‾21‾ ‾19‾ ‾5‾ ‾19‾

   ‾19‾ ‾12‾ ‾5‾ ‾5‾ ‾16‾ ‾9‾ ‾14‾ ‾7‾   ‾19‾ ‾9‾ ‾3‾ ‾11‾ ‾14‾ ‾5‾ ‾19‾ ‾19‾.

6. Comoros: ‾1‾   ‾16‾ ‾5‾ ‾18‾ ‾6‾ ‾21‾ ‾13‾ ‾5‾   ‾3‾ ‾15‾ ‾13‾ ‾5‾ ‾19‾   ‾6‾ ‾18‾ ‾15‾ ‾13‾

   ‾20‾ ‾8‾ ‾5‾   ‾25‾ ‾12‾ ‾1‾ ‾14‾ ‾7‾ - ‾25‾ ‾12‾ ‾1‾ ‾14‾ ‾7‾   ‾20‾ ‾18‾ ‾5‾ ‾5‾.

7. Congo's rain forest people: ‾20‾ ‾18‾ ‾1‾ ‾22‾ ‾5‾ ‾12‾   ‾9‾ ‾14‾   ‾4‾ ‾21‾ ‾7‾ ‾15‾ ‾21‾ ‾20‾

   ‾3‾ ‾1‾ ‾14‾ ‾15‾ ‾5‾ ‾19‾.

8. Gambia (James Island):   ‾23‾ ‾1‾ ‾19‾   ‾15‾ ‾14‾ ‾3‾ ‾5‾   ‾1‾

   ‾19‾ ‾12‾ ‾1‾ ‾22‾ ‾5‾ - ‾20‾ ‾18‾ ‾1‾ ‾4‾ ‾9‾ ‾14‾ ‾7‾   ‾3‾ ‾5‾ ‾14‾ ‾20‾ ‾5‾ ‾18‾.

^ ^

Name _____ Date _____

NUMBER CODE
KENYA THROUGH TANZANIA

A - 1	G - 7	M - 13	S - 19	Y - 25
B - 2	H - 8	N - 14	T - 20	Z - 26
C - 3	I - 9	O - 15	U - 21	
D - 4	J - 10	P - 16	V - 22	
E - 5	K - 11	Q - 17	W - 23	
F - 6	L - 12	R - 18	X - 24	

DIRECTIONS

Look at the numbers under each line. Find the matching numbers in the code box and write the letters on the corresponding answer lines.

1. Kenya: ___ ___ ___ ___ ___ - ___ ___ ___ ___ ___ ___   ___ ___ ___   ___ ___ ___
   23 15 18 12 4 - 6 1 13 15 21 19   6 15 18   9 20 19

   ___ ___ ___ ___   ___ ___ ___ ___ ___ ___ ___
   23 9 12 4   1 14 9 13 1 12 19

2. Liberia: ___ ___ ___ ___ ___ ___ ___   ___ ___   ___ ___ ___ ___
   6 15 21 14 4 5 4   2 25   19 15 13 5

   ___ ___ ___ ___ ___ ___ ___ ___ ___   ___ ___   ___   ___ ___ ___ ___
   1 13 5 18 9 3 1 14 19   1 19   1   8 15 13 5

   ___ ___ ___   ___ ___ ___ ___ ___   ___ ___ ___ ___ ___ ___
   6 15 18   6 18 5 5 4   19 12 1 22 5 19

3. Madagascar: ___ ___ ___   ___ ___ ___ ___   ___   ___ ___ ___ ___ ___ ___ ___ ___
   23 1 19   15 14 3 5   1   6 1 22 15 18 9 20 5

   ___ ___ ___ ___   ___ ___ ___   ___ ___ ___   ___ ___ ___ ___ ___ ___
   2 1 19 5   6 15 18   19 5 1   16 9 18 1 20 5 19

4. Morocco (Bidonvilles): ___ ___ ___ ___ - ___ ___ ___ ___ ___   ___ ___ ___ ___ ___
   19 12 21 13 - 8 15 13 5   1 18 5 1 19

   ___ ___ ___ ___ ___   ___ ___ ___ ___   ___ ___ ___   ___ ___ ___ ___ ___
   2 21 9 12 20   23 9 20 8   20 9 14   3 1 14 19

5. Niger: ("___ ___ ___ ___   ___ ___ ___ ___ ___ ___ ___")   ___ ___ ___ ___ ___ ___
   (" 20 5 14 20   19 3 8 15 15 12 19")   6 15 12 12 15 23

   ___ ___ ___ ___ ___ ___ ___   ___ ___ ___ ___ ___ ___
   14 15 13 1 4 9 3   20 18 9 2 5 19

6. Seychelles: ___ ___ ___ ___ ___   ___ ___ ___ ___ ___ ___ ___ ___ ___;
   7 9 1 14 20   20 15 18 20 15 9 19 5 19;

   ___ ___ ___ ___ ___ ___   ___ ___ ___ ___ ___ ___ ___ ___
   4 15 21 2 12 5   3 15 3 15 14 21 20 19   50 pounds

   ___ ___ ___ ___ ___   ___ ___ ___ ___ ___
   23 5 9 7 8   1 2 15 21 20

7. Sierra Leone: ___ ___ ___ ___ ___ ___ ___ ___   ___ ___ ___ ___ ___   ___ ___
   4 9 1 13 15 14 4 19   6 15 21 14 4   9 14

   ___ ___ ___ ___ ___ ___   ___ ___ ___   ___ ___ ___ ___ ___ ___ ___ ___
   19 23 1 13 16 19   1 14 4   18 9 22 5 18 2 5 4 19

8. Tanzania (Africa's highest mountain): ___ ___ ___ ___ ___ ___ ___ ___ ___ ___ ___ ___
   11 9 12 9 13 1 14 10 1 18 15

Ostrich

Dama Gazelle

^ ^

AFRICA MOUNTAINS

^ ^

Name _____ Date _____

R	J	O	R	A	J	N	A	M	I	L	I	K
A	E	A	T	A	H	A	T	C	E	L	O	C
G	B	M	D	Y	G	A	R	O	C	A	T	A
G	E	K	V	N	C	A	N	Y	G	B	N	B
A	L	O	S	E	P	E	A	C	A	R	F	D
H	D	R	A	K	E	N	S	B	E	R	G	P
A	U	F	L	S	D	N	A	L	H	G	I	H
L	E	R	T	I	B	E	S	T	I	B	R	C
E	T	M	A	S	S	I	F	W	I	R	U	E
B	A	J	K	M	F	S	L	O	E	I	W	N
O	R	T	U	T	E	B	H	P	V	E	E	G
M	A	K	O	U	S	S	I	I	V	A	N	A
B	B	D	R	R	Q	N	R	L	H	K	Z	P
O	M	U	O	S	U	U	A	R	A	S	O	M
D	U	I	N	J	N	C	R	W	F	D	R	A
V	S	N	H	G	M	A	S	M	P	J	I	H
J	U	S	A	W	N	O	O	R	E	M	A	C

Mt. Kilimanjaro

WORD SEARCHING
DIRECTIONS

This grid contains hidden words. The hidden words appear in bold print in the list to the right. They can go up, down, across, at an angle, forward, or backward.

Ahaggar (Mts., Sahara Desert)

(Aïr) **Massif** (Mts., Sahara Desert)

Atacora (Mt., Benin)

Atlas (Mt., Morocco)

Cameroon (Mt., Cameroon)

Champagne (Castle Mt., S. Africa)

Drakensberg (Mts., S. Africa)

(Emil) **Koussi** (Mts., Sahara Desert)

(Ethiopian) **Highlands** (Ethiopia)

Jebel (Toubkal Mt., Morocco)

Juniper (Mt., Algeria)

Lebombo (Mts., Swaziland)

(Mt.) **Kenya** (Kenya)

(Mt.) **Kilimanjaro** (Tanzania)

(Mt.) **Tahat** (Algeria)

Ras (Dashen Mt., Ethiopia)

Ruwenzori (Range, Zaire)

(Sierra) **Leone** (Mt., Sierra Leone)

Tibesti (Mt., Sahara Desert)

Usumbara (Mts., Tanzania)

Virunga (Mts., Rwanda)

28

^ ^ ^ ^ ^ ^ ^ ^ ^ ^ ^ ^ ^ ^ ^

Name _____ Date _____

CROSSING OVER

DIRECTIONS

Use a pencil for this game. Find words from the following list (the words not in parentheses) that have the correct number of spaces and letters to fit into the crossing-over boxes. Each word has a place where it belongs. The first word is done for you. To continue, find a 7-letter word with "e" in the fifth space and so on. All the words tell about rivers in Africa.

U M B E L U Z I

4 letters

Baro (Ethiopia)

Blue (Nile, Sudan)

Bomu (C.A. Republic)

(Dire) **Dawa** (Ethiopia)

Nile (world's longest River, Egypt)

Tana (Kenya)

Vaal (S. Africa)

5 letters

Awash (Ethiopia)

(Bahr al) **Jabal** (Sudan)

Benue (Nigeria)

Black (Volta, Ghana)

Chari (Chad)

Congo (a major River, Zaire)

Kasai (Kenya)

Niger (a major R., Nigeria)

Nzoia (Kenya)

6 letters

Atbara (Sudan)

Cacheu (Guinea-Bissau)

Cuango (Angola)

Cuanza (Angola)

Gambia (Senegal)

Kaduna (Nigeria)

Komati (Swaziland)

Kunene (Namibia)

Logone (Chad)

Lomami (Zaire)

Ogooue (Gabon)

Orange (S. Africa)

Ubangi (Congo)

7 letters

Gongola (Nigeria)

Limpopo (S. Africa)

Lualaba (Zaire)

Senegal (Senegal)

Turkwel (Kenya)

Zambezi (Mozambique)

8 letters

Okavango (Namibia)

Umbeluzi (Swaziland)

9 letters

Ingwavuma (Swaziland)

Shabeelle (Somalia)

Casamance (Senegal)

Nile River Farmland

Name _____ Date _____

NUMBER CODE
DIRECTIONS

Look at the number under each line. Find the matching number in the code box. Write the letter that matches that number on the corresponding answer lines.

A - 1	G - 7	M - 13	S - 19	Y - 25
B - 2	H - 8	N - 14	T - 20	Z - 26
C - 3	I - 9	O - 15	U - 21	
D - 4	J - 10	P - 16	V - 22	
E - 5	K - 11	Q - 17	W - 23	
F - 6	L - 12	R - 18	X - 24	

Important national fishing catches:

‾1‾ ‾14‾ ‾3‾ ‾8‾ ‾15‾ ‾22‾ ‾9‾ ‾5‾ ‾19‾

‾3‾ ‾1‾ ‾18‾ ‾16‾

Mackerel

‾13‾ ‾1‾ ‾3‾ ‾11‾ ‾5‾ ‾18‾ ‾5‾ ‾12‾

‾8‾ ‾1‾ ‾11‾ ‾5‾   ‾16‾ ‾5‾ ‾18‾ ‾3‾ ‾8‾

‾19‾ ‾1‾ ‾18‾ ‾4‾ ‾9‾ ‾14‾ ‾5‾ ‾19‾   ‾19‾ ‾8‾ ‾1‾ ‾4‾

‾19‾ ‾1‾ ‾18‾ ‾4‾ ‾9‾ ‾14‾ ‾5‾ ‾12‾ ‾12‾ ‾1‾   ‾19‾ ‾8‾ ‾18‾ ‾9‾ ‾13‾ ‾16‾

‾20‾ ‾21‾ ‾14‾ ‾1‾   ‾18‾ ‾15‾ ‾3‾ ‾11‾   ‾12‾ ‾15‾ ‾2‾ ‾19‾ ‾20‾ ‾5‾ ‾18‾

Some favorite national dishes:

1. ‾1‾ ‾12‾ ‾7‾ ‾5‾ ‾18‾ ‾9‾ ‾1‾:   ‾3‾ ‾15‾ ‾21‾ ‾19‾ ‾3‾ ‾15‾ ‾21‾ ‾19‾

   (‾19‾ ‾20‾ ‾5‾ ‾1‾ ‾13‾ ‾5‾ ‾4‾   ‾23‾ ‾8‾ ‾5‾ ‾1‾ ‾20‾   ‾15‾ ‾18‾

   ‾2‾ ‾1‾ ‾18‾ ‾12‾ ‾5‾ ‾25‾   ‾23‾ ‾9‾ ‾20‾ ‾8‾   ‾13‾ ‾5‾ ‾1‾ ‾20‾,

   ‾22‾ ‾5‾ ‾7‾ ‾5‾ ‾20‾ ‾1‾ ‾2‾ ‾12‾ ‾5‾ ‾19‾,   ‾19‾ ‾1‾ ‾21‾ ‾3‾ ‾5‾)

Sardine

2. Egypt: ‾6‾ ‾5‾ ‾12‾ ‾1‾ ‾6‾ ‾5‾ ‾12‾,   (‾22‾ ‾5‾ ‾7‾ ‾5‾ ‾20‾ ‾1‾ ‾2‾ ‾12‾ ‾5‾ ‾19‾,

   ‾6‾ ‾12‾ ‾15‾ ‾21‾ ‾18‾,   ‾19‾ ‾16‾ ‾9‾ ‾3‾ ‾5‾ ‾19‾,   ‾19‾ ‾1‾ ‾21‾ ‾3‾ ‾5‾,

   ‾19‾ ‾5‾ ‾18‾ ‾22‾ ‾5‾ ‾4‾   ‾9‾ ‾14‾   ‾16‾ ‾9‾ ‾20‾ ‾1‾   ‾2‾ ‾18‾ ‾5‾ ‾1‾ ‾4‾)

3. Senegal: ‾3‾ ‾8‾ ‾9‾ ‾3‾ ‾11‾ ‾5‾ ‾14‾   ‾19‾ ‾20‾ ‾5‾ ‾23‾;   ‾19‾ ‾16‾ ‾9‾ ‾3‾ ‾25‾

   ‾13‾ ‾5‾ ‾1‾ ‾20‾   ‾15‾ ‾18‾   ‾6‾ ‾9‾ ‾19‾ ‾8‾   ‾23‾ ‾9‾ ‾20‾ ‾8‾

   ‾16‾ ‾5‾ ‾1‾ ‾14‾ ‾21‾ ‾20‾   ‾19‾ ‾1‾ ‾21‾ ‾3‾ ‾5‾

4. Ethiopia: ‾23‾ ‾1‾ ‾20‾   (‾1‾   ‾19‾ ‾20‾ ‾5‾ ‾23‾)

Tuna

Name _____ Date _____

CROSSING OVER

DIRECTIONS

Use a pencil for this game. Find words from the following list (the words not in parentheses) that have the correct number of spaces and letters to fit into the crossing-over boxes. Each word has a place where it belongs. The first word is done for you. To continue, find a 7-letter word with "e" in the first space, and so on. All the words tell about deserts, lakes, and special areas in Africa.

3 letters
  (Lake) **Mai** (Ndome)
  Low (Africa region)

4 letters
  High (Africa region)
  (Lake) **Chad**
  (Lake) **Kivu**
  (Lake) **Tana**
  Rift (earth cracks)

5 letters
  Congo (basin area)
  (Lake) **Abaya**
  (Lake) **Mweru**
  (Lake) **Nyasa**
  (Lake) **Volta**
  (Lake) **Ziway**
  (Nile) **Basin** (area)
  Oases (fertile desert areas)

6 letters
  Karibe (Lake)
  (Lake) **Albert**
  (Lake) **Edward**
  (Lake) **Nasser**
  Libyan (Desert)
  Nubian (Desert)
  Sahara (world's largest desert)

7 letters
  Eastern (Highlands area)
  (Lake) **Turkana**
  Savanna (area of grass, shrubs, low trees)
  Western (Plateau area)

8 letters
  (coastal area) **Lowlands**
  Kalahari (Desert)
  (Lake) **Victoria** (Africa's largest)
  Northern (Highlands area)
  Southern (Plateau area)

10 letters
  (Lake) **Tanganyika** (world's longest freshwater lake)

Sahara Desert

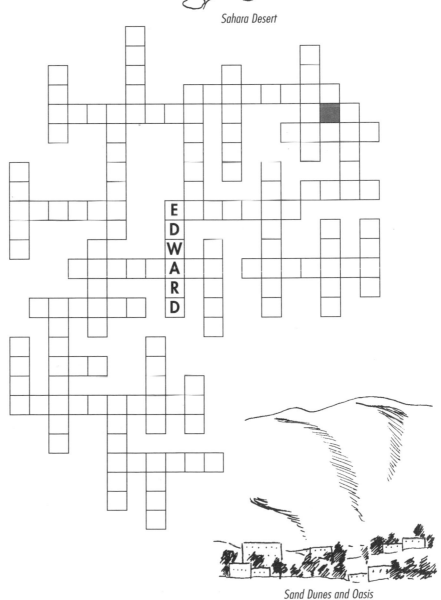

E
D
W
A
R
D

Sand Dunes and Oasis

AFRICA SEAPORTS

Name _____ Date _____

A	K	I	E	D	T	B	A	N	J	U	L	C
B	E	I	R	A	U	O	I	P	M	A	Q	O
L	C	L	M	K	N	D	R	N	A	I	S	T
W	T	O	S	A	I	D	O	B	R	V	R	O
Y	J	B	V	R	S	U	T	Z	A	O	A	N
T	R	I	P	O	L	I	C	S	M	R	B	O
F	C	T	C	D	N	E	I	F	P	N	G	U
G	A	O	A	H	B	L	V	I	A	O	J	K
L	B	I	S	S	A	U	M	H	N	M	O	N
R	I	P	A	W	N	S	I	U	O	L	E	Q
A	D	R	B	S	J	O	T	M	I	U	P	V
S	J	W	L	N	U	G	B	Y	R	B	A	A
M	A	M	A	A	L	A	S	F	E	H	C	L
A	N	D	N	C	S	L	D	O	A	I	G	A
C	U	J	C	A	L	N	P	R	K	S	M	U
S	L	U	A	N	D	A	M	A	P	U	T	O
N	O	D	N	O	L	D	B	N	E	V	Y	D

WORD SEARCHING
DIRECTIONS
Find the names of African seaports hidden in the grid. The hidden words appear in bold print in the list below. They can go up, down, across, at an angle, forward, or backward.

Abidjan (Ivory Coast)
Banjul (Gambia)
Beira (Mozambique)
Bissau (Guinea-Bissau)
Camsar (Guinea)
Cape (Town) (South Africa)
Casablanca (Morocco)
Cotonou (Benin)
Dakar (Senegal)
(Dar es) **Salaam** (Tanzania)
Douala (Cameroon)
(East) **London** (South Africa)
Lagos (Nigeria)
Lobito (Angola)
Luanda (Angola)
Maputo (Mozambique)
Marampa (Sierra Leone)
Mombasa (Kenya)
Monrovia (Liberia)
Oran (Algeria)
(Pointe-) **Noire** (Congo)
(Port) **Louis** (Mauritius)
(Port) **Said** (Egypt)
(Port) **Sudan** (Sudan)
Tripoli (Libya)
Tunis (Tunisia)
Victoria (Seychelles)
Walis (Bay) (Namibia)

Seaport

From *The Continents*, published by GoodYearBooks. Copyright © 1994 Jeanne and Arnold Cheyney.

Name _____ Date _____

NUMBER CODE

DIRECTIONS

Look at the number under each line. Find the matching number in the code box. Write the letter that matches that number on the corresponding answer lines.

A - 1	G - 7	M - 13	S - 19	Y - 25
B - 2	H - 8	N - 14	T - 20	Z - 26
C - 3	I - 9	O - 15	U - 21	
D - 4	J - 10	P - 16	V - 22	
E - 5	K - 11	Q - 17	W - 23	
F - 6	L - 12	R - 18	X - 24	

1. Ethiopia: men and women wear one-piece white cotton garments called __ __ __ __ __ __ __.
   19 8 1 13 13 1 19.

2. Ghana: men wrap in colorful cloths called __ __ __ __ __   __ __ __ __ __.
   11 5 14 20 9   3 12 15 20 8.

3. Morocco: many men wear a red, brimless hat called a __ __ __. A men's loose-fitting, hooded robe is
   6 5 26.

   a __ __ __ __ __ __ __ __. Women wear loose __ __ __ __ __ __ __.
   4 10 5 12 12 1 2 1.   3 1 6 20 1 14 19.

4. Mauritania: women wear a __ __ __ __, a long cloth wrapped around the body.
   19 1 18 9,

5. Egyptian men wear a long, loose garment called a __ __ __ __ __ __ __ __ __.
   7 1 12 1 2 9 25 1 8.

6. Sudan: a garment covering women from head to foot is a __ __ __ __.
   20 1 21 2.

7. Guinea: a man's long, hooded cloak is a __ __ __ __ __ __.
   2 15 21 2 15 21.

8. Algeria: a man's long, hooded cloak is a __ __ __ __ __ __ __ __. Women wear a white-cotton
   2 21 18 14 15 15 19 5.

   outer garment called a __ __ __ __.
   8 1 9 11.

9. Liberia: a long piece of cloth wrapped around the waist, with a blouse or skirt is a __ __ __ __ __.
   12 1 16 16 1.

10. Somalia: traditional men's clothing is a kilt-like garment called a __ __ __ __ __. Some wear a cloth,
    12 21 14 7 9.

    of bright colors, draped like a __ __ __ __.
    20 15 7 1.

Clothing

Clothing

From *The Continents*, published by GoodYearBooks. Copyright © 1994 Jeanne and Arnold Cheyney.

Name _____ Date _____

ALGERIA THROUGH LIBYA

DIRECTIONS

Find the latitude and longitude of each item below by using maps in the encyclopedia or atlas. Write the answers in the blanks to the right.

1. 30° North Latitude, 0° Longitude: __ __ __ __ __ __ __

2. 10° North Latitude, 3° East Longitude: __ __ __ __ __

3. 13° North Latitude, 3° West Longitude: __ __ __ __ __ __ __   __ __ __ __ __

4. 5° North Latitude, 12° East Longitude: __ __ __ __ __ __ __ __

5. 8° North Latitude, 22° East Longitude: __ __ __ __ __ __ __   __ __ __ __ __ __ __
__ __ __ __ __ __ __ __

6. 12° South Latitude, 44° East Longitude: __ __ __ __ __ __ __

7. 12° North Latitude, 43° East Longitude: __ __ __ __ __ __ __

8. 2° North Latitude, 10° East Longitude: __ __ __ __ __ __ __ __   __ __ __ __ __ __

9. Between 13° to 14° North Latitude, 16° West Longitude: __ __ __ __ __ __

10. 10° North Latitude, 12° West Longitude: __ __ __ __ __ __

11. 7° North Latitude, 6° West Longitude: __ __ __ __ __   __ __ __ __ __

12. 30° South Latitude, 28° East Longitude: __ __ __ __ __ __ __

13. 30° North Latitude, 15° East Longitude: __ __ __ __ __

14. 10° South Latitude, 16° East Longitude: __ __ __ __ __ __

15. 20° South Latitude, 25° East Longitude: __ __ __ __ __ __ __ __

16. 3° South Latitude, 30° East Longitude: __ __ __ __ __ __ __

17. 16° North Latitude, 24° West Longitude: __ __ __ __   __ __ __ __ __

18. 15° North Latitude, 20° East Longitude: __ __ __ __

19. 0° Equator, 15° East Longitude: __ __ __ __ __

20. 30° North Latitude, 30° East Longitude: __ __ __ __ __

21. 0° Equator, 12° East Longitude: __ __ __ __ __

22. 8° North Latitude, 1° West Longitude: __ __ __ __ __

23. 12° North Latitude, 15° West Longitude: __ __ __ __ __ __ - __ __ __ __ __ __

24. 0° Equator, 38° East Longitude: __ __ __ __ __

25. 6° North Latitude, 10° West Longitude: __ __ __ __ __ __ __

From *The Continents*, published by GoodYearBooks. Copyright © 1994 Jeanne and Arnold Cheyney.

Name _____ Date _____

MADAGASCAR THROUGH ZIMBABWE

DIRECTIONS

Find the latitude and longitude of each item below by using maps in the encyclopedia or atlas. Write the answers in the blanks to the right.

1. 20° South Latitude, 45° East Longitude: __ __ __ __ __ __ __ __ __ __

2. 16° North Latitude, 0° Longitude: __ __ __ __

3. 20° South Latitude, 57° 40' East Longitude: __ __ __ __ __ __ __ __ __

4. 15° South Latitude, 40° East Longitude: __ __ __ __ __ __ __ __ __

5. 8° North Latitude, 8° East Longitude: __ __ __ __ __ __

6. 0° 30' North Latitude, 6° 30' East Longitude:

   __ __ __   __ __ __ __   and   __ __ __ __ __ __

7. 5° South Latitude, 55° East Longitude: __ __ __ __ __ __ __ __ __

8. 10° North Latitude, 50° East Longitude: __ __ __ __ __ __ __ __

9. 10° North Latitude, 30° East Longitude: __ __ __ __ __

10. 5° South Latitude, 35° East Longitude: __ __ __ __ __ __ __ __

11. 34° North Latitude, 10° East Longitude: __ __ __ __ __ __

12. 0° Equator, 24° East Longitude: __ __ __ __ __

13. 20° South Latitude, 30° East Longitude: __ __ __ __ __ __ __

14. 12° South Latitude, 34° East Longitude: __ __ __ __ __

15. 24° North Latitude, 8° West Longitude: __ __ __ __ __ __ __ __ __

16. 32° North Latitude, 8° West Longitude: __ __ __ __ __ __ __

17. 18° North Latitude, 8° East Longitude: __ __ __ __

18. 2° South Latitude, 30° East Longitude: __ __ __ __ __ __

19. 15° North Latitude, 15° West Longitude: __ __ __ __ __ __

20. 8° North Latitude, 12° West Longitude: __ __ __ __ __   __ __ __ __

21. 30° South Latitude, 25° East Longitude: __ __ __ __ __ __   __ __ __ __

22. Between 26° to 27° South Latitude, and 31° to 32° East Longitude: __ __ __ __ __ __ __ __ __ __

23. 8° North Latitude, 1° East Longitude: __ __ __ __

24. 2° North Latitude, 32° East Longitude: __ __ __ __ __ __

25. 15° South Latitude, 25° East Longitude: __ __ __ __ __

From *The Continents*, published by GoodYearBooks. Copyright © 1994 Jeanne and Arnold Cheyney.

ANTARCTICA

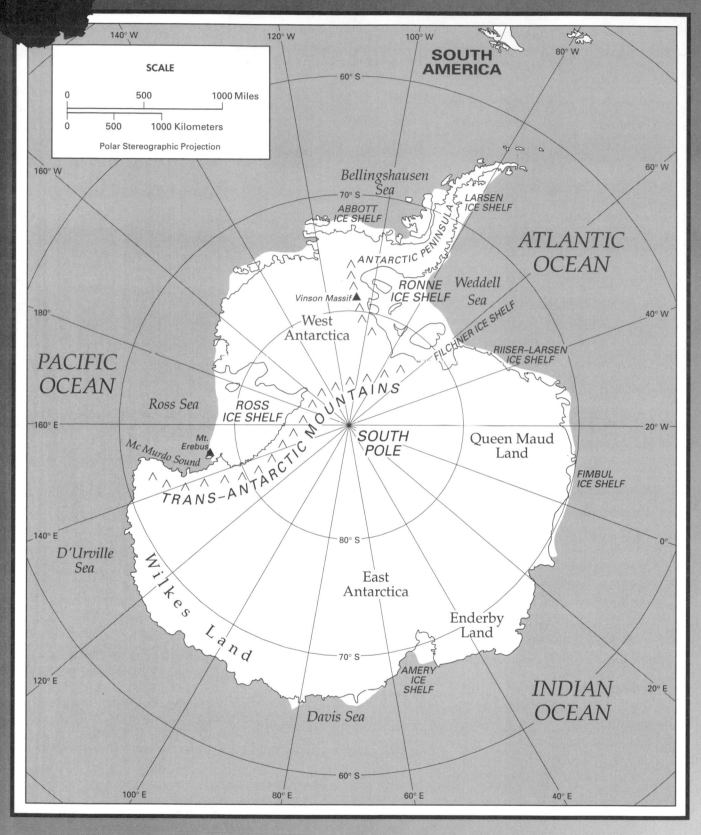

SCALE

| 0 | 500 | 1000 Miles |

| 0 | 500 | 1000 Kilometers |

Polar Stereographic Projection

140° W · 120° W · 100° W · 80° W

SOUTH AMERICA

60° S

160° W

Bellingshausen Sea

70° S

ABBOTT ICE SHELF

LARSEN ICE SHELF

60° W

ANTARCTIC PENINSULA

ATLANTIC OCEAN

180°

Vinson Massif ▲

RONNE ICE SHELF

Weddell Sea

West Antarctica

40° W

FILCHNER ICE SHELF

RIISER–LARSEN ICE SHELF

PACIFIC OCEAN

Ross Sea

ROSS ICE SHELF

TRANS–ANTARCTIC MOUNTAINS

160° E

Mc Murdo Sound

Mt. Erebus ▲

SOUTH POLE

Queen Maud Land

20° W

FIMBUL ICE SHELF

140° E

D'Urville Sea

80° S

East Antarctica

0°

Wilkes Land

Enderby Land

120° E

70° S

AMERY ICE SHELF

20° E

Davis Sea

INDIAN OCEAN

100° E · 80° E · 60° E · 40° E

60° S

From *The Continents*, published by GoodYearBooks. Copyright © 1994 Jeanne and Arnold Cheyney.

^ ^

Name _____ Date _____

24. Most of Antarctica lies under snow and ice _____ mile deep.

DOWN

1. An Antarctic explorer: James Clark _____
2. An Antarctic Explorer: Richard E. _____
3. The South _____ is close to the Ross Ice Shelf.
4. _____ oceans surround Antarctica.
5. An Antarctic bird: Arctic _____
6. _____ Peninsula extends toward South America.
8. A land within the continent: _____ Land
10. An arctic explorer: Robert _____
12. An ocean bordering Antarctica
13. Mt. Erebus: An active _____ on Ross Island
14. West Antarctica faces the Pacific Ocean and _____ America.
15. Two summer plants that grow on hillsides: moss and _____
16. Highest peak in Antarctica: _____ Massif
17. An Antarctic explorer: Robert _____
19. _____ can't grow because they have deep roots.
20. The _____ bird eats penguin eggs and chicks.
21. Midwinter is in _____.

CROSSWORD PUZZLE

ACROSS

3. Hardy _____ and some insects live on a few rocky hillsides.
6. Antarctica is twice the size of _____.
7. A land within the continent: _____ Maud Land
9. An ocean bordering Antarctica
11. A smaller ice shelf facing the South Atlantic Ocean
18. Many _____ deposits lie along the coast facing the Indian Ocean and in the mountains.
22. Barren _____ with exposed rocks surround most of the continent's edge.
23. An ocean bordering Antarctica

Penguins

From *The Continents*, published by GoodYearBooks. Copyright © 1994 Jeanne and Arnold Cheyney.

^ ^

ASIA

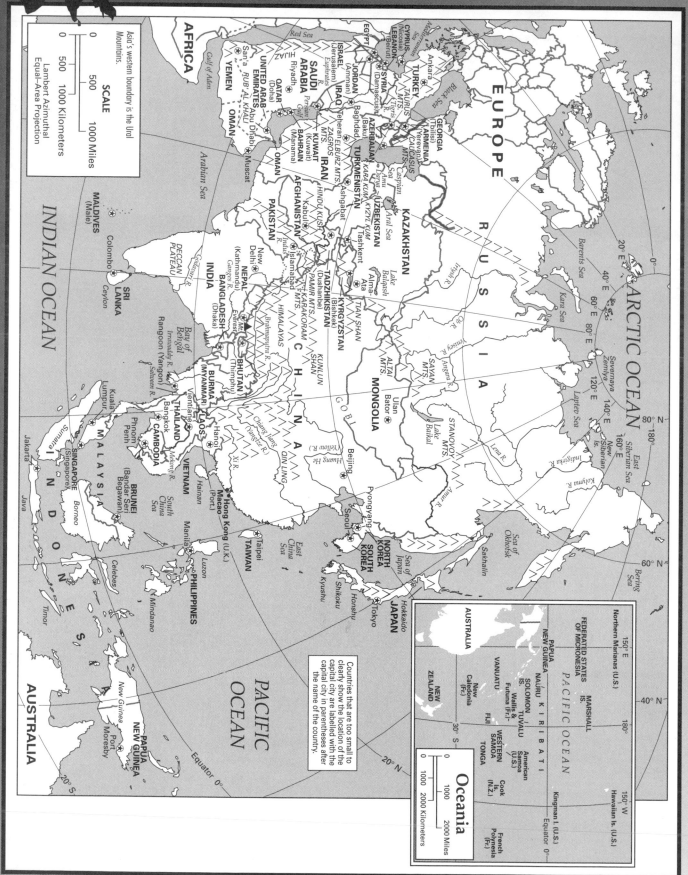

SCALE

Asia's western boundary is the Ural Mountains.

Lambert Azimuthal Equal-Area Projection

0   500   1000 Kilometers
0   500   1000 Miles

AFRICA

EUROPE

ARCTIC OCEAN

R U S S I A

INDIAN OCEAN

PACIFIC OCEAN

AUSTRALIA

Red Sea
Gulf of Aden
YEMEN
San'a
RUB' AL KHALI
OMAN
Muscat
Arabian Sea
MALDIVES (Male)
INDIAN OCEAN
SRI LANKA (Ceylon)
Colombo

EGYPT
CYPRUS (Nicosia)
LEBANON (Beirut)
ISRAEL (Jerusalem)
JORDAN (Amman)
SAUDI ARABIA
Riyadh
UNITED ARAB EMIRATES
Abu Dhabi
QATAR (Doha)
BAHRAIN (Manama)
Persian Gulf
KUWAIT (Kuwait)
IRAQ
Baghdad
SYRIA (Damascus)
TURKEY
Ankara
Euphrates R.
Tigris R.
TAURUS MTS.
Mediterranean Sea
HIJAZ
Tehran
IRAN
ELBURZ MTS.
ZAGROS MTS.
GEORGIA (Tbilisi)
ARMENIA (Yerevan)
AZERBAIJAN (Baku)
CAUCASUS MTS.
Black Sea
Caspian Sea
KARA KUM
TURKMENISTAN
Ashgabat
AFGHANISTAN
Kabul
HINDU KUSH
PAKISTAN
Islamabad
Indus R.
UZBEKISTAN
Tashkent
KYZYL KUM
Aral Sea
TADZHIKISTAN (Dushanbe)
PAMIR MTS.
KARAKORUM
KYRGYZSTAN (Bishkek)
TIAN SHAN
KAZAKHSTAN
Alma Ata
Lake Balkash
ALTAI MTS.
SAYAN MTS.
Ob R.
Yenisey R.
Angara R.
Lake Baikal
STANOVOY MTS.

New Delhi
INDIA
DECCAN PLATEAU
Cauvery R.
NEPAL (Kathmandu)
Ganges R.
Mt. Everest
BHUTAN (Thimphu)
HIMALAYAS
Brahmaputra R.
BANGLADESH (Dhaka)
Bay of Bengal
BURMA (MYANMAR) (Rangoon (Yangon))
Irrawaddy R.
Salween R.
KUNLUN SHAN
QIN LING
CHINA
GOBI
MONGOLIA
Ulan Bator
Huang He (Yellow R.)
Chang Jiang (Yangtze R.)
Xi R.
Beijing
Hainan
VIETNAM
Hanoi
LAOS (Vientiane)
THAILAND
Bangkok
CAMBODIA
Phnom Penh
Mekong R.
South China Sea
Macao
Hong Kong (U.K.)
East China Sea
TAIWAN
Taipei
PHILIPPINES
Manila
Luzon
Mindanao
MALAYSIA
Kuala Lumpur
SINGAPORE (Singapore)
BRUNEI (Bandar Seri Begawan)
Borneo
Sumatra
Jakarta
INDONESIA
Java
Celebes
Timor
New Guinea

NORTH KOREA
Pyongyang
SOUTH KOREA
Seoul
Sea of Japan
JAPAN
Tokyo
Hokkaido
Honshu
Kyushu
Shikoku
Sakhalin
Sea of Okhotsk
Amur R.
Kolyma R.
Indigirka R.
Lena R.
Laptev Sea
New Siberian Is.
East Siberian Sea
Bering Sea
Severnaya Zemlya
Kara Sea
Barents Sea

PAPUA NEW GUINEA
Port Moresby
AUSTRALIA
PACIFIC OCEAN
Equator 0°
20° N
40° N
60° N
80° N
20° S
0°
20° E
40° E
60° E
80° E
120° E
140° E
160° E
180°

Countries that are too small to clearly show the location of the capital city are labeled with the capital city in parentheses after the name of the country.

Oceania

AUSTRALIA

NEW ZEALAND
New Caledonia (Fr.)
VANUATU
SOLOMON IS.
Wallis & Futuna (Fr.)
TUVALU
FIJI
American Samoa (U.S.)
WESTERN SAMOA (U.S.)
TONGA
Cook Is. (N.Z.)
French Polynesia (Fr.)
K I R I B A T I
NAURU
MARSHALL IS.
FEDERATED STATES OF MICRONESIA
Northern Marianas (U.S.)
PAPUA NEW GUINEA
PACIFIC OCEAN
Kingman I. (U.S.)
Hawaiian Is. (U.S.)
Equator 0°
40° N
30° S
20° S
150° E
160° E
180°
150° W

0   1000   2000 Kilometers
0   1000   2000 Miles

Name _____ Date _____

CROSSWORD PUZZLE

ACROSS

1. People who move from place to place with herds of animals
3. Asia covers one-_____ of the world's land area.
4. S.W. Asia: a world exporter of _____ (liquid mineral)
6. A chief river
7. China and Tibet: the only places where the Giant _____ lives in the wild
8. A large south, southeast wild animal (monkey-like)
9. Asians established the first _____.
11. A chief grain crop
12. A tamed northern work-animal used for food, clothing, shelter
14. Most farmers live in small _____ (places).
15. Southern end of Asia located in the _____ (near equator)
17. Northern tip lies within the _____ Circle.
24. World's highest mountain range
26. A chief crop
28. Lowest place on earth's surface: _____ Sea shore
29. World's highest mountain

Going to Market

DOWN

2. Asia: more _____ than any continent
5. Asians devised the first system of _____.
10. World's largest inland sea
13. Much of S.E. Asia is _____.
16. Asians were the first _____ (occupation) and merchants.
18. Asians invented _____ (form of communication).
19. Nomad tribal leaders are called _____.
20. Asians invented _____ (tool for communication).
21. Large northern animal (south of Arctic area)
22. Longest Asian river
23. Three-fifths of people _____ for a living.
25. Civilization _____ in Asia.
27. World's largest _____ and pine trees (south of Arctic)

From *The Continents*, published by GoodYearBooks. Copyright © 1994 Jeanne and Arnold Cheyney.

Name _____ Date _____

AFGHANISTAN THROUGH LAOS CROSSWORD PUZZLE

ACROSS

1. Country north of Saudi Arabia; east of Israel
4. Country east of Iraq; west of Afghanistan
5. Country nearly surrounded by India; at the northern tip of the Bay of Bengal
7. Country west of Iran; northeast of Saudi Arabia
8. Country north and east of Thailand; west of Vietnam
9. Country northwest of Jordan; west of Syria
10. Country north of India; south of Mongolia
12. Country southwest of China; southeast of Pakistan
13. Country northeast of India; southwest of China
14. Country south of North Korea; west of southern Japan: _____ Korea
15. Country on the north of Borneo island; surrounded by Malaysia
16. Country north of South Korea; northeast of China: North _____
17. Island country in the Mediterranean Sea; south of Turkey
18. Country at the northern end of the Persian Gulf; south of Iraq

DOWN

1. Country east and north of South Korea; east of the Sea of Japan
2. Country east of Saudi Arabia; north of Qatar
3. Country (formerly called Kampuchea) west of Vietnam; southeast of Thailand
6. Country east of Iran; north of Pakistan
11. Country (islands) northwest of Australia; south and east of Malaysia
15. Country west of Thailand; east of Bhutan on the Bay of Bengal

Carrying Water

From *The Continents*, published by GoodYearBooks. Copyright © 1994 Jeanne and Arnold Cheyney.

CAPITALS OF INDEPENDENT COUNTRIES **ASIA**

Name _____ Date _____

AFGHANISTAN THROUGH LAOS
CROSSWORD PUZZLE

ACROSS

4. Capital of Indonesia (Asian)
7. Capital of Bhutan
8. Capital of Brunei: _____ Seri Begawan
12. Capital of Israel
14. Capital of Japan
16. Capital of Kuwait
17. Capital of Burma
18. Capital of Korea (South)
19. Capital of China
20. Capital of Bahrain

DOWN

1. Capital of Iraq
2. Capital of Bangladesh
3. Capital of Iran
5. Capital of Jordan
6. Capital of Cambodia: Phnom _____
9. Capital of Afghanistan
10. Capital of India: New _____
11. Capital of (North) Korea
13. Capital of Laos
15. Capital of Cyprus

Old and New

From *The Continents*, published by GoodYearBooks. Copyright © 1994 Jeanne and Arnold Cheyney.

Name _____ Date _____

LEBANON THROUGH YEMEN CROSSWORD PUZZLE

ACROSS

3. Country northwest of India; south of Afghanistan
4. Country southeast of Saudi Arabia; east of Yemen
5. Country west of Vietnam; south of Laos
8. Tiny country at the southern tip of the Malay Peninsula; northeast of Sumatra
9. Country northeast of India; west of Bhutan
13. Country east of Thailand; east of Cambodia (formerly Kampuchea)
14. Island country at the southern tip of India; east of Maldives: _____ Lanka
16. Country in the Arabian Peninsula; north of Yemen and Oman: _____ Arabia
17. Country bordering the Mediterranean Sea on the east; north of Syria and Iraq
18. Country west of Syria; bordering the Mediterranean Sea

DOWN

1. Country north of China; south of Russia
2. A country (peninsula) jutting out into the Persian Gulf; east of Saudi Arabia and southeast of Bahrain
3. Country (of many islands) east of Vietnam; south of Taiwan
6. Country north of Jordan; east of Israel
7. Country (peninsula and islands) south of Asia; northwest of Australia
10. Island country north of the Philippines; east of China
11. Country (of many islands) in the Indian Ocean; south of India
12. Country north of Oman; south of Qatar: United _____ Emirates
15. Country southwest of Saudi Arabia; west of Oman

Common Transportation

Malaysia

From *The Continents*, published by GoodYearBooks. Copyright © 1994 Jeanne and Arnold Cheyney.

CAPITALS OF INDEPENDENT COUNTRIES ASIA

Name _____ Date _____

LEBANON THROUGH YEMEN CROSSWORD PUZZLE

ACROSS

2. Capital of Qatar
3. Capital of Thailand
5. Capital of Nepal
7. Capital of Yemen
8. Capital of the Philippines
9. Capital of Saudi Arabia
13. Capital of Sri Lanka
15. Capital of Syria
16. Capital of Taiwan
17. Capital of Turkey
18. Capital of Lebanon

DOWN

1. Capital of Pakistan
2. Capital of United Arab Emirates: Abu _____
4. Capital of Malaysia: _____ Lumpur
6. Capital of Maldives
10. Capital of Vietnam
11. Capital of Singapore
12. Capital of Oman
14. Capital of Mongolia: Ulan _____

Aden, Yemen

^ ^

Name _____ Date _____

CROSSING OVER

DIRECTIONS

Use a pencil for this game. Find words from the following list (the words not in parentheses) that have the correct number of spaces and letters to fit into the crossing-over boxes. Each word has a place where it belongs. The first word is done for you. To continue, find a 7-letter word with "m" in the fourth space, and so on. All the words name wild animals.

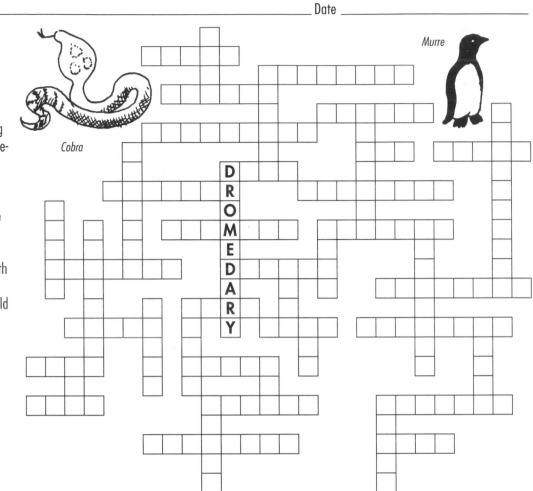

Cobra

Murre

D
R
O
M
E
D
A
R
Y

3 letters

ape

(Arctic) **fox**

elk

yak (tamed work animal)

4 letters

anoa (small buffalo)

(Arabian) **oryx** (antelope)

(Arctic) **hare**

(Baikal hair) **seal**

gaur (ox)

ibex (goat)

lynx (cat family)

musk (deer)

(water) **deer**

5 letters

(Bactrian) **camel**

(Bengal) **tiger**

brown (bear)

(cobra) **snake**

(Giant) **panda**

(Malay) **tapir**

murre (sea bird)

orang(utang)

sable

(wild) **horse**

6 letters

ermine (weasel)

gibbon (ape-like)

(komodo) **dragon**

onager (ass)

(Rhesus) **monkey**

7 letters

caracal (lynx)

karakul (sheep)

leopard

peacock

(rodent) **lemming**

tarsier (large eyes, long tail)

(water) **buffalo**

8 letters

antelope

elephant

(golden) **pheasant** (bird)

hornbill (tropical bird)

mongoose (ferret-like)

reindeer

scorpion

9 letters

crocodile

dromedary

10 letters

rhinoceros

Giant Panda

^ ^

From *The Continents*, published by GoodYearBooks. Copyright © 1994 Jeanne and Arnold Cheyney.

Name _____ Date _____

O	A	I	D	P	F	C	L	B	T	M	S	P
J	L	P	R	A	X	K	T	A(○)	H	W	U	
R	M	(○)	L	L	E	T	R	Y	A	E	W	N
Q	C	N	V	M	B	R	R	Q	O	C	T	S
E	S	E	N	E	T	L	E	Z	X	I	V	S
H	E	A	U	B	S	Y	K	B	T	T	A	E
V	O	P	G	F	E	M	J	O	B	R	T	N
G	W	P	I	B	K	A	R	A	G	(○)	S	L
Q	S	L	U	H	L	S	M	F	J	S	R	P
C	O	E	D	R	Y	H	E	G	S	K	O	A
V	C	N	W	B	N	J	D	T	N	T	E	N
D	C	P	C	O	Y	E	L	R	(○)	B	O	H
C	A	R	T	E	D	I	U	T	E	D	Q	S
C	B	T	W	Q	E	D	O	F	B	U	F	G
I	(○)	A	T	S	M	E	L	S	Y	C	T	J
C	T	R	H	T	S	W	A	J	O	R	B	I
P	V	G	N	E	P	O	T	V	S	C	B	K

SUPPLY THE VOWEL

DIRECTIONS

This grid contains hidden words. The hidden words appear in bold print in the list below. The words can go up, down, across, at angles, backward, or forward. Parts of words may overlap. Supply the correct vowel—a e i o u—for the center of each word group.

barley
citrus (fruit)
corn
cotton
dates
jute (burlap)
millet
oats
olives
pineapple
potatoes
rice
rubber
rye
soybeans
(sugar) **beets**
sugar (cane)
tea
tobacco
wheat

Planting Rice

Name _____ Date _____

WORD SEARCHING

DIRECTIONS

This grid contains hidden words. The hidden words appear in bold print in the list below. They can go up, down, across, at an angle, forward, or backward.

Plants:

bamboo

kudzu

jute (for burlap)

myrrh

tea

turmeric

Date Palm

Eastern Spruce

Jute

Trees:

banyan

beech

betel (palm)

Cedar (of Lebanon)

cinnamon

date (palm)

dawn (redwood)

(Eastern) **fir**

(Eastern) **spruce**

frankincense

gingko

loquat (fruit)

mango (fruit tree)

nutmeg

olive

padauk

rattan

rubber

teak

tung (for oil)

(white) **mulberry** (leaves for silkworms)

Frankincense

A	H	C	G	E	B	E	T	E	L	H	G	F
B	E	E	C	H	W	U	N	A	T	T	A	R
S	I	D	R	Y	D	E	O	D	A	R	I	A
D	K	A	E	T	Z	Y	D	T	F	V	C	N
M	J	R	B	F	I	R	P	A	D	A	U	K
S	T	U	B	K	A	R	A	W	E	V	B	I
C	R	N	U	T	M	E	G	V	Q	X	P	N
G	U	D	R	A	T	B	I	O	R	T	Z	C
N	Z	C	B	U	A	L	E	Q	J	U	T	E
U	C	I	P	Q	O	U	T	P	B	R	J	N
T	N	N	O	O	B	M	A	B	T	M	Y	S
E	K	N	P	L	I	H	D	A	E	E	G	E
C	E	A	P	I	N	E	Q	N	O	R	N	K
U	J	M	Y	R	R	H	M	Y	L	I	D	D
R	F	O	G	N	A	M	R	A	F	C	S	A
P	M	N	L	K	N	G	I	N	K	G	O	W
S	L	T	R	A	G	A	C	A	N	T	H	N

Name _____   Date _____

CROSSING OVER

DIRECTIONS

Use a pencil for this game. Find words from the following list (the words not in parentheses) that have the correct number of spaces and letters to fit into the crossing-over boxes. Each word has a place where it belongs. The first word is done for you. To continue, find a 7-letter word with "p" in the fourth space, and so on. All the words name places in Asia.

2 letters
(Huang) **He**
Ob
Xi

3 letters
Amu (Darya)
Red (River)

4 letters
Amur
Aral (Sea) (a lake)
Dead (Sea) (a lake)
Lena

5 letter
Black (Sea)
(East) **China** (Sea)
Indus
Jiang
Kolym
Karun
Menam
(Sea of) **Japan**
South (China Sea)

6 letters
Angara
Bering (Sea)
Ganges
Irtysh
Jordan
(Lake) **Baikal**
Mekong
Tigris

7 letters
Arabian (Sea)
Caspian (Sea)
Helmand
Okhotsk (Sea)
Salween
Yangtze
Yenisey

8 letters
Godavari
(Lake) **Balkhash**

9 letters
Euphrates
Indigirka
Irrawaddy

11 letters
Brahmaputra

Dead Sea

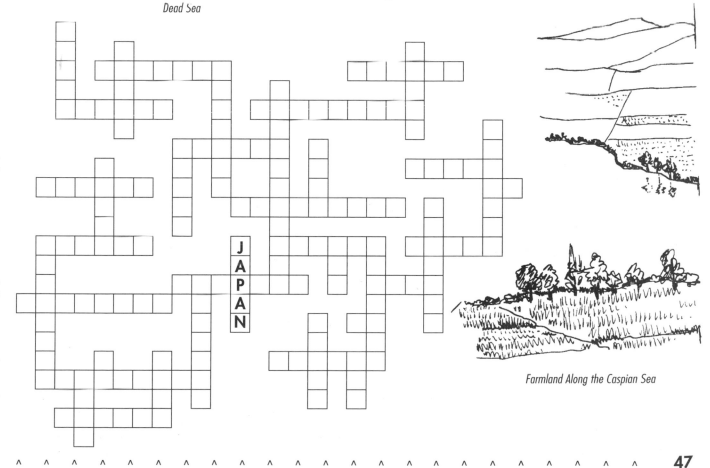

Farmland Along the Caspian Sea

MOUNTAINS AND DESERTS

Name _____ Date _____

Himalaya (snow-capped)

SUPPLY THE VOWEL
DIRECTIONS

This grid contains hidden words. The hidden words appear in bold print in the list below. The words can go up, down, across, at angles, backward, or forward. Parts of words may overlap. Supply the correct vowel—a e i o u—for the center of each word group.

Mountains:
- Altai
- Elburz
- Himalaya
- (Hindu) **Kush**
- Karakoram
- Kunlun
- Lebanon
- (Mount) **Everest**
- Pamir
- Qilian
- Qin (Ling)
- Stanovoy
- **Taurus**
- Tian (Shan)
- Zagros

Deserts:
- Gobi
- Kara (Kum)
- (Kyzyl) **Kum**
- Negev
- (Rub al) **Khali**

A	K	C	L	G	P	F	J	G	Y	S	U	B
D	I	H	N	K	A	R	A	K	O	R	A	M
M	K	Z	O	L	T	A	I	R	V	B	W	T
H	Q	R	I	L	O	N	G	S	O	E	I	A
B	A	E	L	D	I	A	K	C	N	J	I	V
K	N	G	I	M	Z	T	F	L	A	N	Q	H
T	O	R	Q	V	B	R	W	P	T	O	Y	S
Z	A	N	M	A	R	E	U	F	S	N	I	C
H	S	O	K	S	R	H	O	B	C	A	K	U
L	K	L	R	N	D	W	M	J	L	B	N	G
V	T	N	D	U	B	E	V	E	R	O	S	T
Z	G	U	Y	I	S	K	H	Q	G	L	P	A
U	O	K	S	B	R	P	O	E	A	Q	X	J
N	E	S	L	N	D	A	V	H	Y	U	P	K
C	L	T	E	P	A	M	N	J	Q	W	G	V
A	Y	A	L	A	M	O	H	N	C	V	R	A
M	F	D	M	T	Q	R	T	I	U	B	W	F

China

From *The Continents*, published by GoodYearBooks. Copyright © 1994 Jeanne and Arnold Cheyney.

Name _____ Date _____

NUMBER CODE
DIRECTIONS

Look at the number under each line. Find the matching number in the code box. Write the letter that matches that number on the corresponding answer lines.

A - 1	G - 7	M - 13	S - 19	Y - 25
B - 2	H - 8	N - 14	T - 20	Z - 26
C - 3	I - 9	O - 15	U - 21	
D - 4	J - 10	P - 16	V - 22	
E - 5	K - 11	Q - 17	W - 23	
F - 6	L - 12	R - 18	X - 24	

1. Afghanistan has no ___ ___ ___ ___ ___ ___ ___ ___ .
   19 5 1 3 15 1 19 20

2. ___ ___ ___ ___ is on the west border.
   9 18 1 14

3. The country on the south and southeast border: ___ ___ ___ ___ ___ ___ ___ ___
   16 1 11 9 19 20 1 14

4. Capital and largest city: ___ ___ ___ ___ ___ .
   11 1 2 21 12

5. Most workers ___ ___ ___ ___ the land or ___ ___ ___ ___ ___ ___ ___ ___ ___ ___ ___ ___ ___
   6 1 18 13   18 1 9 19 5   12 9 22 5 19 20 15 3 11

6. Most people live in ___ ___ ___ - ___ ___ ___ ___ ___ ___ ___ ___ ___ .
   13 21 4   2 18 9 3 11   8 15 13 5 19

7. Most semi-nomads live in ___ ___ ___ ___ - ___ ___ ___ ___ ___ ___ ___ ___ ___ .
   7 15 1 20   8 1 9 10   20 5 14 20 19

8. Islam house of worship: ___ ___ ___ ___ ___ ___
   13 15 19 17 21 5

9. At every meal, Afghans eat ___ ___ ___ ___ ___ ___ ___ ___ ___ ___ ___ ___
   6 12 1 20   12 15 1 22 5 19   15 6
   ___ ___ ___ ___ ___ .
   2 18 5 1 4

10. Favorite drink: ___ ___ ___
    20 5 1

11. Famous dogs: ___ ___ ___ ___ ___ ___   ___ ___ ___ ___ ___ ___
    1 6 7 8 1 14   8 15 21 14 4 19

12. Few people 15 and older can ___ ___ ___ ___   ___ ___   ___ ___ ___ ___ ___
    18 5 1 4   15 18   23 18 9 20 5

13. Chief crop: ___ ___ ___ ___ ___
    23 8 5 1 20

14. Some areas have ___ ___ ___ ___ ___ ___ ___ ___ ___ ___ to produce ___ ___ ___ ___
    9 18 18 9 7 1 20 9 15 14   13 15 18 5
    ___ ___ ___ ___ .
    6 15 15 4

15. Some crops: ___ ___ ___ ___ , ___ ___ ___ ___ ___ , ___ ___ ___ ___ ,
    18 9 3 5   6 18 21 9 20   3 15 18 14
    ___ ___ ___ ___ ___ ___ , ___ ___ ___ ___ ___ , ___ ___ ___ ___ ___
    3 15 20 20 15 14   2 1 18 12 25   14 21 20 19

Village Schoolboy

Winnowing Grain

From *The Continents*, published by GoodYearBooks. Copyright © 1994 Jeanne and Arnold Cheyney.

ASIA **BURMA**

Name _____ Date _____

NAME AN IMPORTANT RIVER
DIRECTIONS

Fill in the dotted lines with your answers. If they are correct, the circled letters will spell the name of an important river in Burma.

1. Most important form of transportation

2. Capital and largest city

3. Most people 15 and older can _____.

4. Most people are _____ (occupation).

5. Important tree

6. Houses are made of

7. Due to _____ and wild animals, houses are built on poles.

8. Precious stones mined

9. Most rain falls from _____ to October.

Ducks

Preparing Food

BURMA PAIRS OF CROPS AND FOODS
DIRECTIONS

All of the crop and food names in the rectangle are written twice, except for one. Write the name of each crop and food pair once on a blank. (Cross off the pairs as you find them.) Then find the name of Burma's chief food, which appears only once, and write it in the box.

vegetables
fruit
garlic
shrimp
rice
corn
cotton
bananas
onions
sesame
peanuts
sesame
jute
cotton
tobacco
wheat
fruit
durians
millet
millet
sugar
vegetables
onions
citrus
rubber
fish
bananas
durians
peanuts
chicken
fish
corn
sugar
shrimp
rubber
tobacco
jute
chicken
citrus
wheat
garlic

chief crop

50

From *The Continents*, published by GoodYearBooks. Copyright © 1994 Jeanne and Arnold Cheyney.

Name _____ Date _____

From *The Continents*, published by GoodYearBooks. Copyright © 1994 Jeanne and Arnold Cheyney.

DOWN

1. First country to develop _____
2. The Chinese place a high value on _____.
4. Eating utensils
6. A food (from soybean curds)
7. High towers with turned-up roof edges
12. World's most heavily populated city
13. Huang He means "yellow _____."
14. Newer popular food: ice _____
15. Poultry product
16. China: some of the world's best _____ land
18. South China's favorite food

CROSSWORD PUZZLE

ACROSS

1. World's chief producer of sweet _____ (vegetable)
3. Famous landmark: Great _____ of China
5. Popular poultry food in the North
8. World's largest producer of _____ (fruit)
9. Nearly all families raise _____ (farm animals).
10. China has the world's largest _____.
11. Important occupation: _____ farming
14. Important vegetable
17. Northern grain crop (for bread)
19. A beverage
20. Most common means of transportation in cities
21. Capital

Hoeing Sweet Potatoes

Name _____ Date _____

NUMBER CODE
DIRECTIONS

Look at the number under each line. Find the matching number in the code box. Write the letter that matches that number on the corresponding answer lines.

A - 1	G - 7	M - 13	S - 19	Y - 25
B - 2	H - 8	N - 14	T - 20	Z - 26
C - 3	I - 9	O - 15	U - 21	
D - 4	J - 10	P - 16	V - 22	
E - 5	K - 11	Q - 17	W - 23	
F - 6	L - 12	R - 18	X - 24	

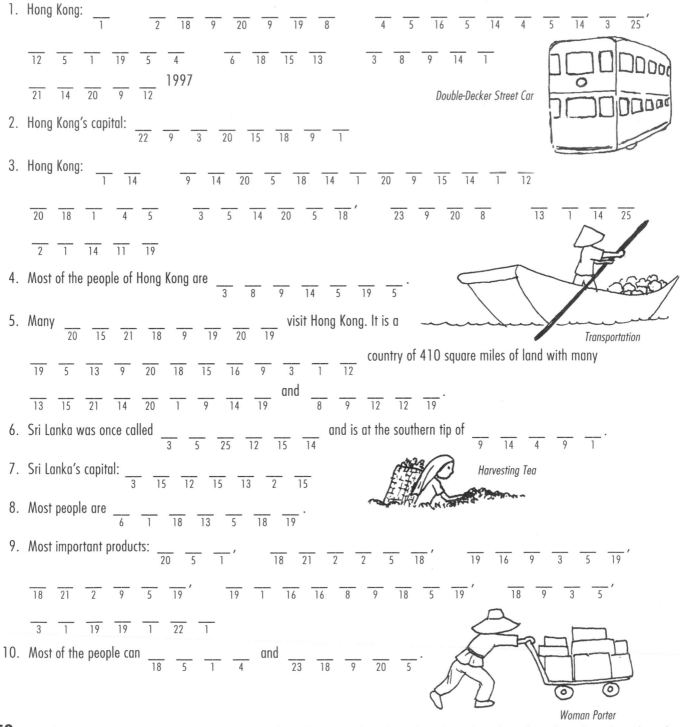

1. Hong Kong: __ __ __ __ __ __ __ __   __ __ __ __ __ __ __ __ __ __'
1   2 18 9 20 9 19 8   4 5 16 5 14 4 5 14 3 25

__ __ __ __ __ __   __ __ __ __   __ __ __ __ __
12 5 1 19 5 4   6 18 15 13   3 8 9 14 1

__ __ __ __ __ 1997
21 14 20 9 12

Double-Decker Street Car

2. Hong Kong's capital: __ __ __ __ __ __ __ __
22 9 3 20 15 18 9 1

3. Hong Kong: __ __   __ __ __ __ __ __ __ __ __ __ __ __ __ __
1 14   9 14 20 5 18 14 1 20 9 15 14 1 12

__ __ __ __ __   __ __ __ __ __ __'   __ __ __ __   __ __ __ __
20 18 1 4 5   3 5 14 20 5 18   23 9 20 8   13 1 14 25

__ __ __ __ __
2 1 14 11 19

4. Most of the people of Hong Kong are __ __ __ __ __ __ __.
3 8 9 14 5 19 5

5. Many __ __ __ __ __ __ __ __ visit Hong Kong. It is a
20 15 21 18 9 19 20 19

__ __ __ __ __ __ __ __ __ __ __ country of 410 square miles of land with many
19 5 13 9 20 18 15 16 9 3 1 12

__ __ __ __ __ __ __ __ __ and __ __ __ __ __.
13 15 21 14 20 1 9 14 19   8 9 12 12 19

6. Sri Lanka was once called __ __ __ __ __ __ and is at the southern tip of __ __ __ __ __.
3 5 25 12 15 14   9 14 4 9 1

7. Sri Lanka's capital: __ __ __ __ __ __ __
3 15 12 15 13 2 15

Harvesting Tea

8. Most people are __ __ __ __ __ __ __.
6 1 18 13 5 18 19

9. Most important products: __ __ __,   __ __ __ __ __ __,   __ __ __ __ __ __,
20 5 1   18 21 2 2 5 18   19 16 9 3 5 19

__ __ __ __ __ __,   __ __ __ __ __ __ __ __ __,   __ __ __ __,
18 21 2 9 5 19   19 1 16 16 8 9 18 5 19   18 9 3 5

__ __ __ __ __ __ __
3 1 19 19 1 22 1

10. Most of the people can __ __ __ __ and __ __ __ __ __.
18 5 1 4   23 18 9 20 5

Woman Porter

From *The Continents*, published by GoodYearBooks. Copyright © 1994 Jeanne and Arnold Cheyney.

Name _____ Date _____

CROSSING OVER

DIRECTIONS

Use a pencil for this game. Find words from the following list (the words not in parentheses) that have the correct number of spaces and letters to fit into the crossing-over boxes. Each word has a place where it belongs. The first word is done for you. To continue, find a 5-letter word with "t" in the fifth space, and so on. All the words tell about India.

3 letters

dal (seed porridge)

hot

(most village houses) **mud**

tea

4 letters

clay (water pots)

deer

milk

(most important) **rail** (road transportation)

rice (main crop)

(women) **sari** (wrapped cloth)

5 letters

brass (cooking pots)

caste (social class)

curry (spicy food)

(New) **Delhi** (capital)

(season) **rainy** (June to September)

slums

(Taj) **Mahal** (tomb)

tiger

wheat (a main crop)

6 letters

Bombay (largest city)

cattle (many)

cotton

Ganges (R.)

Ghandi (led India to independence)

grains (food crops)

school (most villages)

Many Clothing Styles

Farmer

7 letters

buffalo (gives most milk)

chutney (relish)

(Great) **Britain** (once ruled)

monkeys

monsoon (severe winds)

tandoor (clay oven)

8 letters

earrings (popular)

elephant

(location) **southern** (Asia)

(most people live in) **villages**

(world's highest) **Himalaya** (Mts.)

9 letters

bracelets (popular)

(most) **marriages** (arranged)

(red or black dots on) **foreheads** (kumkum)

11 letters

Brahmaputra (R.)

Name _____ Date _____

A	N	D	Q	R	G	S	H	T	A	B	C	M
I	K	A	H	I	L	F	R	U	I	T	N	B
O	R	Q	R	C	U	S	O	E	A	R	P	S
I	Z	J	S	E	S	F	P	H	T	O	L	N
L	E	G	T	W	H	D	Y	O	I	O	V	B
M	K	Y	U	A	A	E	Q	B	O	L	C	D
Y	S	O	N	T	H	D	T	H	M	F	W	A
T	H	G	I	E	W	L	C	J	N	A	E	T
I	F	U	B	R	C	S	T	E	A	R	L	E
C	V	R	A	K	H	O	M	E	I	N	I	S
I	B	T	R	Y	G	H	W	L	S	Z	E	F
R	T	U	L	B	A	Z	A	A	R	B	V	N
T	W	H	E	A	T	K	B	R	E	A	D	A
C	A	T	Y	N	O	I	S	Q	P	L	Y	E
E	K	Z	V	I	S	I	T	I	N	G	W	B
L	V	R	U	P	L	E	N	T	I	L	S	A
E	J	V	E	G	E	T	A	B	L	E	S	M

Weaving Leaves

WORD SEARCHING

DIRECTIONS

This grid contains hidden words. The hidden words appear in bold print in the list that follows. They can go up, down, across, at an angle, forward, or backward.

barley

bazaar (market place)

bean (soup)

(boys, girls separate) **schools**

bread (a chief food)

dates (crop)

(famous) **Persian** (rugs)

(favorite pastime) **visiting**

floor (used as table for meals in rural areas)

fruit (eat lots)

(Iran; east of) **Iraq**

Khomeini (led revolt, became leader)

lamb (a chief food)

lentils (crop)

(most villages, no running) **water**

(most villages, no) **electricity**

(name for king) **shah**

nuts (crop)

oil (wells)

rice (a chief food)

(sport) **weight** (lifting)

tea

Teheran (capital)

vegetables (a chief food)

(villages, public) **baths**

wheat

(women cover faces with a) **veil**

yogurt (a chief food)

Name _____ Date _____

NAME THE RIVER
DIRECTIONS

Fill in the dotted lines with your answers. If they are correct, the circled letters will spell a river's name.

*Iraqi
Woman*

1. A desert animal used for transportation
2. Second largest group of people
3. Many desert herders have flocks of _____.
4. Capital
5. An important river
6. Most Iraqis are _____ (occupation).
7. Some Iraqis have herds of animals in the _____.
8. Most important port
9. Many village homes are made of mud _____.

1. _ _ _ ◯ _
2. _ ◯ _ _ _
3. _ _ _ _ ◯
4. _ _ _ _ ◯
5. _ _ _ ◯ _
6. _ ◯ _ _ _ _ _
7. _ _ _ _ ◯ _
8. ◯ _ _ _ _ _ _
9. _ _ _ _ _ ◯

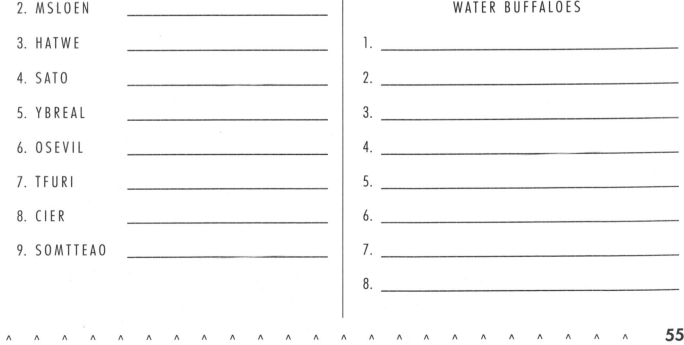

SCRAMBLED CROPS
DIRECTIONS

Unscramble the words and write the answers on the lines provided. (Use scrap paper to work out your answers.)

1. A S E D T _____
2. M S L O E N _____
3. H A T W E _____
4. S A T O _____
5. Y B R E A L _____
6. O S E V I L _____
7. T F U R I _____
8. C I E R _____
9. S O M T T E A O _____

WORDS IN WORDS
DIRECTIONS

How many words of 4 or more letters can you make from the letters in "water buffaloes," work animals raised in Iraq? There are at least 50 words. Use each letter only once. Do not use plurals. Do not use proper nouns.

WATER BUFFALOES

1. _____
2. _____
3. _____
4. _____
5. _____
6. _____
7. _____
8. _____

Name _____ Date _____

CROSSWORD PUZZLE

ACROSS

1. Chief commerce center: Tel _____
4. A chief dairy product
6. Capital and largest city
7. Israel: a large part of the Bible's _____ Land
8. Jewish immigrants turned useless land into _____ land.
11. A chief fruit
13. Climate: _____ summers, cool winters
17. Israel: most _____ Middle Eastern country
18. Nazareth (largest town): where _____ lived as a boy
21. Near Dead Sea: heat evaporates water rapidly, leaving _____
23. Two official languages: _____ and Arabic
24. Chief farm crops: _____ fruits

Menorah

DOWN

1. Minority population
2. 1948: Jews named their country _____.
3. Very important industry: cutting imported _____ (gem)
5. With irrigation, crops now grow in the _____ Desert.
9. A chief farm product
10. Longest river
12. In a _____, farmers share labor and property.

14. Place where Jesus lived most of his life
15. _____ Sea: salty lake shore is world's lowest land
16. A chief grain crop
19. Country west of Israel
20. Mount _____: highest mountain
22. Most of the people are _____ (nationality).

Orthodox Jews

From *The Continents*, published by GoodYearBooks. Copyright © 1994 Jeanne and Arnold Cheyney.

Name _____   Date _____

CROSSING OVER

DIRECTIONS

Use a pencil for this game. Find words from the following list (the words not in parentheses) that have the correct number of spaces and letters to fit into the crossing-over boxes. Each word has a place where it belongs. The first word is done for you. To continue, find an 8-letter word with "r" in the third space, and so on. All the words tell about Japan.

3 letters
tea

4 letters
eggs
(highest mts.) **Alps**
hogs
judo
(most important) **fish**
(most important) **rice**
(Mt.) **Fuji** (highest peak)
(straw) **mats** (floor cover)
sumo (wrestling)
tuna

5 letters
(city) **parks**
(indoor) **paper** (walls)
(Japanese attack) **Pearl** (Harbor)
pears
(remove) **shoes** (before entering house)
Tokyo (capital)

6 letters
karate
(lady's) **kimono** (robe)
(largest island) **Honshu**
shrimp
(walled) **garden** (in many homes)

7 letters
cabbage
(children show) **respect** (for authority)
emperor (ruler)
(four big) **islands** (many small)
monsoon (severe winds)
oranges
(some) **farmers**

8 letters
(mountain) **terraces** (some crops)
(rivers) **irrigate** (farms)

9 letters
(many) **volcanoes**
(modern) **apartment** (buildings)
(mostly) **mountains** (and hills)
(some) **fishermen**

10 letters
(a leading) **industrial** (nation)
chopsticks (utensils)

11 letters
(many) earthquakes

12 letters
strawberries

S T R A W B E R R I E S

Kimono

Name _____ Date _____

NUMBER CODE
DIRECTIONS

Look at the number under each line. Find the matching number in the code box. Write the letter that matches that number on the corresponding answer lines.

A - 1	G - 7	M - 13	S - 19	Y - 25
B - 2	H - 8	N - 14	T - 20	Z - 26
C - 3	I - 9	O - 15	U - 21	
D - 4	J - 10	P - 16	V - 22	
E - 5	K - 11	Q - 17	W - 23	
F - 6	L - 12	R - 18	X - 24	

1. Location: southeast of ___ ___ ___ ___ ; northeast of ___ ___ ___ ___ ___ ___ ___ ___ ___ ___ ___
9 18 1 17 ; 19 1 21 4 9 1 18 1 2 9 1 .

2. Kuwait: ___ ___ ___ ___ ___ ___ ___ ___ ___ ___ ___ ___ ___ ___
1 23 15 18 12 4 12 5 1 4 5 18 9 14
___ ___ ___ ___ ___ ___ ___ ___ ___ ___ ___ ___ ___ ___ ___ ___ ___ ___ ___
16 5 20 18 15 12 5 21 13 16 18 15 4 21 3 20 9 15 14

3. Kuwait: one of the ___ ___ ___ ___ ___ ' ___ ___ ___ ___ ___ ___ ___
23 15 18 12 4 19 18 9 3 8 5 19 20
___ ___ ___ ___ ___ ___ ___ ___ ___
3 15 21 14 20 18 9 5 19

4. Free ___ ___ ___ ___ ___ ___ ___ ___ ___ , ___ ___ ___ ___ ___ ___
5 4 21 3 1 20 9 15 14 , 8 5 1 12 20 8
___ ___ ___ ___ ___ ___ ___ , ___ ___ ___ ___ ___ ___ ___ ___ ___ ___ ___
19 5 18 22 9 3 5 , 14 15 9 14 3 15 13 5 20 1 24

5. Largest city: ___ ___ ___ ___ ___ ___ ___
8 1 23 1 12 12 9

6. The ruler is called an ___ ___ ___ ___ .
5 13 9 18 .

7. Kuwait borders the ___ ___ ___ ___ ___ ___ ___ ___ ___ ___ ___ .
16 5 18 19 9 1 14 7 21 12 6 .

8. Climate: ___ ___ ___ from ___ ___ ___ ___ ___ to ___ ___ ___ ___ ___ ___ ___ ___ ___
8 15 20 1 16 18 9 12 19 5 16 20 5 13 2 5 18

9. There are no ___ ___ ___ ___ ___ ___ in Kuwait.
18 9 22 5 18 19

10. Most drinking water is ___ ___ ___ ___ ___ ___ ___ ___ ___ ___ ___ ___ ___ ___
4 9 19 20 9 12 12 5 4 15 3 5 1 14
___ ___ ___ ___ ___ .
23 1 20 5 18 .

11. Kuwait government: ___ ___ ___ ___ ___ ___ ___ ___ ___ ___ ___ ___ ___ ___ ___ ___ ___ ___
20 21 18 14 9 14 7 4 5 19 5 18 20 9 14 20 15
___ ___ ___ ___ ___ ___ ___ ___ ___ ___ ___ ___ ___ ___ ___ ___ ___ ___ ___ ___
6 1 18 13 12 1 14 4 2 25 9 18 18 9 7 1 20 9 15 14

12. 1934: with the ruler's permission, ___ ___ ___ ___ ___ ___ ___ ___ ___ ___ and ___ ___ ___ ___ ___ ___ ___
1 13 5 18 9 3 1 14 19 2 18 9 20 9 19 8
drilled and found much ___ ___ ___ .
15 9 12 .

Kuwait Woman

Camels

Water Sports

From *The Continents*, published by GoodYearBooks. Copyright © 1994 Jeanne and Arnold Cheyney.

Name _____ Date _____

WORD SEARCHING

DIRECTIONS

This grid contains hidden words. The hidden words appear in bold print in the list below. They can go up, down, across, at an angle, forward, or backward.

cacao (tree; seeds for cocoa)

(capital, largest city: Kuala) **Lumpur**

(chief food) **rice**

cobra

crocodile

deer

ebony (tree)

elephant

fig (tree)

fish (important food)

fruits

(head of state) **king**

kampongs (farm settlements)

lizard

(Malaysia divided into parts) **two**

monkey

Pahang (River)

palm (tree)

pepper (crop)

Perak (River)

pigs

pineapple

(popular) **puppet** (dramas)

shrimp (coastal catch)

(swampy, coastal tree) **mangrove**

tiger

(tree) **rubber**

tropical (climate)

vegetables

(a wet monsoon brings heavy) **rain**

(wild) **oxen**

(wrapped skirts for men and women) **sarongs**

O	W	T	A	K	L	G	R	E	B	B	U	R
I	H	R	A	I	N	T	Y	N	O	B	E	I
E	D	O	K	N	W	B	M	F	A	O	N	Q
L	X	P	G	G	S	Y	S	A	C	S	V	T
E	C	I	R	C	G	B	G	N	A	H	A	P
P	F	C	D	J	N	J	N	E	C	R	P	S
H	E	A	R	C	O	I	O	S	M	I	M	U
A	H	L	U	M	P	U	R	G	F	M	O	Q
N	F	G	P	L	M	K	A	I	R	P	N	R
T	K	V	E	U	A	T	S	P	U	S	K	A
W	A	Y	P	Z	K	H	R	T	I	G	E	R
K	R	A	P	P	U	P	P	E	T	B	Y	B
V	E	G	E	T	A	B	L	E	S	F	C	O
R	P	J	R	E	L	I	D	O	C	O	R	C
E	A	D	R	A	Z	I	L	D	E	X	I	G
E	L	P	P	A	E	N	I	P	L	E	H	M
D	M	A	N	G	R	O	V	E	O	N	S	N

Transportation

Name _____ Date _____

CROSSING OVER

DIRECTIONS

Use a pencil for this game. Find words from the following list (the words not in parentheses) that have the correct number of spaces and letters to fit into the crossing-over boxes. Each word has a place where it belongs. The first word is done for you. To continue, find a 7-letter word with "k" in the fourth space, and so on. All the words tell about the Philippines.

3 letters
hot (climate)

4 letters
hogs
(much) **corn**
(much) **rice**
palm (trees)
pine

5 letters
abaca (fibers for rope)
birds (tropical)
Luzon (largest island)
mango (fruit)
(named for Philip II of) **Spain**
sugar (cane)

6 letters
bamboo (houses)
banana (crop)
island (country; many islands)
Manila (capital)
potato (crop)
snakes
(south of) **Taiwan**
(United) **States** (once ruled)

7 letters
carabao (water buffalo-like; work animal)
cassava (root crop)
monkeys
poultry
tarsier (small; owl-like eyes)
tobacco
(tropical) **forests**

8 letters
coconuts
(many) **typhoons**
(taxis are called) **jeepneys**

9 letters
(many) **fishermen**
(people are called) **Filipinos**
(people prize an) **education**
volcanoes (many active)

10 letters
crocodiles
pineapples

11 letters
(frequent) **earthquakes**

Boy

S N A K E S

Raking Salt

60

From *The Continents*, published by GoodYearBooks. Copyright © 1994 Jeanne and Arnold Cheyney.

Name _____ Date _____

NAME THE SOURCE OF WEALTH

DIRECTIONS

Fill in the dotted lines with your answers. If they are correct, the circled letters will spell Saudi Arabia's source of wealth.

1. Most young _____ who go to colleges in other countries study in the United States.
2. Many rural farmers live in fertile desert areas called
3. Much of Saudi Arabia is a vast
4. Capital
5. Boys and girls go to separate
6. City people like radio and
7. People who follow herds and live in tents
8. Persian Gulf port that handles most oil exports: Ras _____
9. Important fishing catch

1. ◯ _ _ _ _ _
2. _ _ _ ◯ _
3. _ _ _ _ ◯
4. ◯ _ _ _ _ _
5. _ _ _ _ ◯ _
6. _ _ _ ◯ _ _ _ _
7. _ _ _ ◯ _ _ _
8. _ _ _ ◯ _
9. _ _ _ _ ◯ _

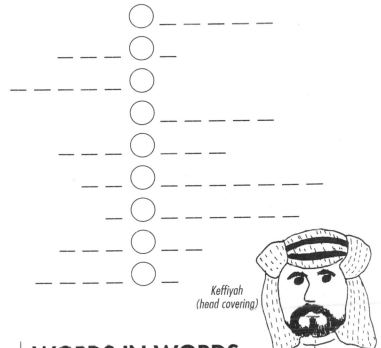

Keffiyah (head covering)

SCRAMBLED FOODS

DIRECTIONS

Unscramble the words and write the answers on the lines provided. (Use scrap paper to work out your answers.)

1. CERI _____
2. UFSTRI _____
3. ASDTE _____
4. EMTA _____
5. BMLA _____
6. HTWAE _____
7. BGTVSEEAEL _____
8. MKLI _____
9. EECSEH _____
10. FECFOE _____

WORDS IN WORDS

DIRECTIONS

How many words can you make from the letters in "Asir Tihamah Mountains," a highland area bordering the western coast?

ASIR TIHAMAH MOUNTAINS

1. _____
2. _____
3. _____
4. _____
5. _____
6. _____
7. _____
8. _____
9. _____

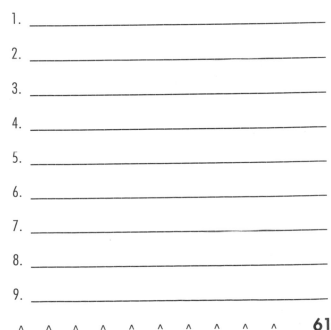

ASIA SOUTH KOREA

^ ^

Name _____ Date _____

NAME AN IMPORTANT FISH

DIRECTIONS

Fill in the dotted lines with your answers. If they are correct, the circled letters will spell the name of an important fish in South Korea.

1. There is _____ of religion.   1. Ⓞ _ _ _ _ _ _

2. Most important food   2. _ Ⓞ _ _

3. Capital and largest city   3. _ _ _ _ Ⓞ

4. The Korean alphabet has _____ letters.   4. _ _ _ Ⓞ _

5. The central mountains are covered mostly with   5. Ⓞ _ _ _ _ _ _

6. A popular food dish made of Chinese cabbage and other vegetables   6. _ Ⓞ _ _ _ _

7. Strong summer wind from the southwest, bringing hot, humid weather   7. _ _ _ Ⓞ _

8. Hurricane-type summer wind (Western Pacific)   8. _ _ _ _ Ⓞ _ _

SKYSCRAPER

DIRECTIONS

Write your answers in the boxes. The circled letters will help you.

1. Most farmers _____ the land they farm.

2. Common farm animal

3. An important river

4. Common seafood

5. Poultry product

6. People _____ their government leaders.

7. A fruit crop

8. A vegetable crop

9. A grain crop

10. Longest river

11. Korea has one of the world's fastest-growing _____.

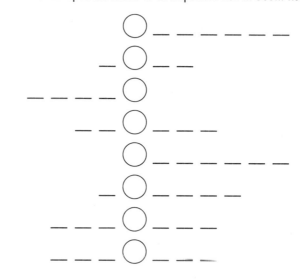

Heron

Grandfather Stone

6. Ⓛ
7. Ⓛ
8. Ⓘ

62

^ ^

From *The Continents*, published by GoodYearBooks. Copyright © 1994 Jeanne and Arnold Cheyney.

Name _____ Date _____

WORD SEARCHING

DIRECTIONS

This grid contains hidden words. The hidden words appear in bold print in the list below. They can go up, down, across, at an angle, forward, or backward.

(an) **ancient** (land)

camel (caravans once carried goods)

(capital, largest city) **Damascus**

cattle

(a chief crop) **cotton**

(chief food) **bread**

(cover much of Syria) **deserts**

(a crop) **barley**

(a crop: sugar) **beets**

(a crop) **wheat**

(favorite drink) **coffee**

(a favorite recreation) **television**

goats

(important river for irrigation) **Euphrates**

(many rural houses: sundried) **mud**

(many rural people live in) **villages**

(most common transportation) **bus**

(nomads who follow herds) **bedouins**

olives

(people like to) **visit**

(prized cloth, dating to ancient times) **brocade**

(rich farmland around) **Orontos** (R.)

sheep

(some of world's oldest) **cities**

(some rural homes made of) **stone**

(source of wealth) **oil**

(Syria had the first) **alphabet**

(west border) **Mediterranean** (Sea)

A	G	E	G	C	M	Q	E	L	T	T	A	C
C	O	F	F	E	E	B	P	D	A	E	R	B
D	A	S	I	L	D	J	F	S	D	H	R	E
K	T	T	N	E	I	C	N	A	T	M	U	D
N	S	O	U	M	T	Y	C	Z	V	C	D	O
A	I	N	O	W	E	O	I	L	B	O	E	U
E	J	E	S	T	R	E	S	E	D	T	C	I
U	H	L	K	B	R	Q	F	G	T	T	S	N
P	S	U	C	S	A	M	A	D	E	O	E	S
H	N	Q	S	O	N	T	L	M	L	N	G	U
R	O	L	I	V	E	S	P	P	E	Y	A	V
A	C	W	H	E	A	T	H	C	V	A	L	Y
T	I	S	I	V	N	C	A	B	I	W	L	E
E	T	T	R	E	H	M	B	U	S	D	I	L
S	I	E	I	G	E	K	E	L	I	K	V	R
F	E	E	M	L	S	O	T	N	O	R	O	A
M	S	B	S	H	E	E	P	O	N	S	J	B

Beehive-shaped Houses

Name _____   Date _____

NUMBER CODE

DIRECTIONS

Look at the number under each line. Find the matching number in the code box. Write the letter that matches that number on the corresponding answer lines.

A - 1	G - 7	M - 13	S - 19	Y - 25
B - 2	H - 8	N - 14	T - 20	Z - 26
C - 3	I - 9	O - 15	U - 21	
D - 4	J - 10	P - 16	V - 22	
E - 5	K - 11	Q - 17	W - 23	
F - 6	L - 12	R - 18	X - 24	

1. Taiwan was formerly called __ __ __ __ __ __ __ .
   6 15 18 13 15 19 1

2. __ __ __ __ __   __ __ __ __ __ __ __ cover about half the island.
   20 8 9 3 11   6 15 18 5 19 20 19

3. Capital __ __ __ __ __ __
   20 1 9 16 5 9

4. __ __ __ __ __ __ __ __   __ __ __ __ __ __ are short and swift.
   13 15 21 14 20 1 9 14   18 9 22 5 18 19

5. The climate is __ __ __   __ __ __   __ __ __ __ __ .
   8 15 20   1 14 4   8 21 13 9 4

6. __ __ __ __ __ __ __ __ do much damage.
   20 25 16 8 15 15 14 19

7. __ __ __ : __ __ __ __ __ __ __ __ __
   2 21 19   5 24 3 5 12 12 5 14 20
   __ __ __ __ __ __ __ __ __ __ __ __ __ __
   20 18 1 14 19 16 15 18 20 1 20 9 15 14

8. Workers wear __ __ __ __ __ __ __   __ __ __ __ __   __ __ __ __ .
   16 15 9 14 20 5 4   19 20 18 1 23   8 1 20 19

9. Some chief crops: __ __ __ __ , __ __ __ , __ __ __ __ __ __ __ __ __ ,
   18 9 3 5   20 5 1   1 19 16 1 18 1 7 21 19
   __ __ __ __ __ __   __ __ __ __ __ __ , __ __ __ __ __ __ __ __ ,
   3 9 20 18 21 19   6 18 21 9 20 19   13 21 19 8 18 15 15 13 19
   __ __ __ __ __ __ __ ,   __ __ __ __ __ __ __ __ __ __ ,
   16 5 1 14 21 20 19   22 5 7 5 20 1 2 12 5 19
   __ __ __ __ ,   __ __ __ __ __ __ __ __ __ __
   3 15 18 14   16 9 14 5 1 16 16 12 5

10. Nearly everyone __ __ __   __ __ __ __   __ __ __   __ __ __ __ __ .
    3 1 14   18 5 1 4   1 14 4   23 18 9 20 5

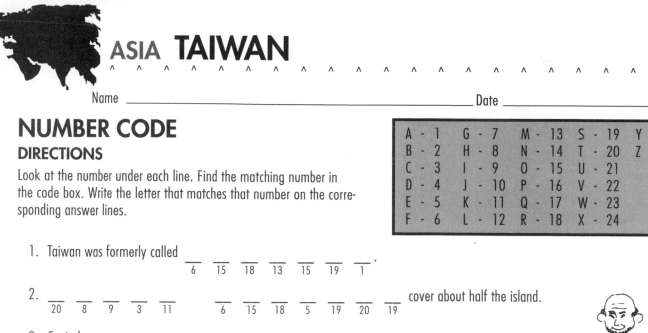

Grandfather

Drying Rice   *Fishing*   *Drying Grain*

From *The Continents*, published by GoodYearBooks. Copyright © 1994 Jeanne and Arnold Cheyney.

Name _____   Date _____

SUPPLY THE VOWEL

DIRECTIONS

This grid contains hidden words. The hidden words appear in bold print in the list below. The words can go up, down, across, at angles, backward, or forward. Parts of words may overlap. Supply the correct vowel—a e i o u—for the center of each word group.

Weaving   *Herding*   *Picking Cotton*

barley

(best farmland) **western** (valleys)

(capital) **Ankara**

(a chief food) **yogurt**

citrus (fruits)

coffee (a favorite drink)

corn

cotton

(cracked-wheat) **bread** (favorite)

(crop) **nuts**

(famous food) **shish** (kabobs)

(favorite food) **rice** (with mutton)

goats

(in two continents, Europe and) **Asia**

(large minority group) **Kurds**

(largest city) **Istanbul**

olives

(popular dessert) **baklava**

sheep

tea (a favorite drink)

D	H	A	R	F	C	L	E	O	M	S	A	F
K	N	B	B	J	I	P	C	L	H	B	D	O
A	N	K	◯	R	A	V	R	◯	C	E	K	M
G	R	S	K	R	Q	U	S	V	T	I	W	C
T	I	B	L	G	L	H	L	E	A	R	T	O
A	J	H	A	R	Y	E	P	S	E	J	U	N
S	N	U	V	C	G	C	Y	B	T	S	I	S
F	D	K	A	C	◯	T	T	O	N	W	W	H
E	M	U	O	F	A	R	Z	M	Q	E	G	C
S	P	W	F	I	T	B	N	P	L	S	K	A
L	C	E	T	S	S	R	Y	N	E	T	A	L
H	E	J	I	T	N	P	A	D	A	◯	R	B
V	F	R	D	A	Y	E	S	O	T	R	H	L
U	W	S	Z	N	J	D	C	D	S	N	I	S
G	B	G	T	B	R	K	F	W	M	U	T	R
F	Y	O	G	◯	R	T	T	O	B	S	H	A
M	P	E	K	L	N	V	I	N	H	D	E	Y

Name _____ Date _____

NAME THE COUNTRIES THAT ONCE RULED

DIRECTIONS

Fill in the dotted lines with your answers. If they are correct, the circled letters will spell the countries that once ruled Vietnam.

1. Many coastal people are _____ (occupation).
2. Northern Highlands have _____ and jungles.
3. Capital
4. Vietnam borders the south _____ Sea.
5. Chief crop
6. Many wear sandals made from old _____.

1. A crop: _____ (for making burlap)
2. The Mekong River Delta is good _____ land.
3. The climate is _____.
4. Most people are _____ (occupation).
5. Largest city

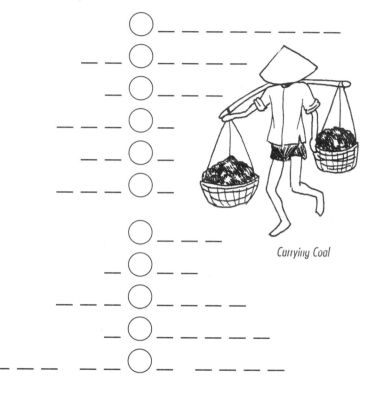

Carrying Coal

VIETNAM SKYSCRAPER

DIRECTIONS

Write your answers in the boxes. The circled letters will help you.

1. Beverage crop
2. Important northern river
3. A chief food
4. Mountains extending nearly the length of Vietnam
5. A root crop
6. A food crop
7. A food crop: sweet _____
8. A crop from a palm tree

Village

Street Car

AUSTRALIA

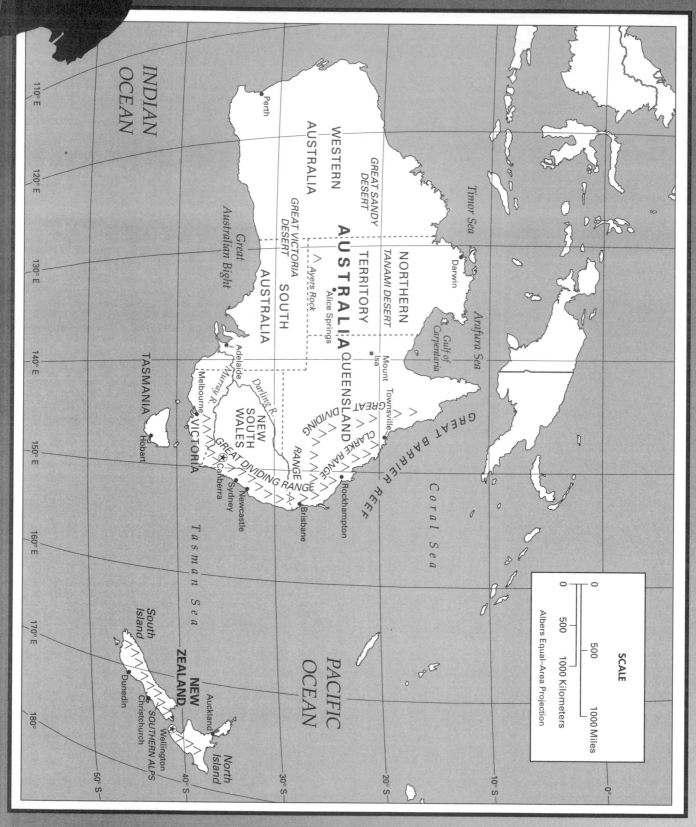

INDIAN OCEAN

Perth

WESTERN AUSTRALIA

GREAT SANDY DESERT

NORTHERN TERRITORY

TANAMI DESERT

Darwin

Timor Sea

GREAT VICTORIA DESERT

AUSTRALIA

Ayers Rock

Alice Springs

Arafura Sea

Gulf of Carpentaria

Great Australian Bight

SOUTH AUSTRALIA

Mount Isa

QUEENSLAND

Townsville

Coral Sea

Adelaide

Murray R.

Darling R.

NEW SOUTH WALES

CLARKE RANGE

GREAT DIVIDING RANGE

Rockhampton

GREAT BARRIER REEF

Melbourne

VICTORIA

GREAT DIVIDING RANGE

Canberra

Sydney

Newcastle

Brisbane

TASMANIA

Hobart

Tasman Sea

PACIFIC OCEAN

South Island

NEW ZEALAND

North Island

Auckland

Dunedin

Christchurch

SOUTHERN ALPS

Wellington

110° E
120° E
130° E
140° E
150° E
160° E
170° E
180°

10° S
20° S
30° S
40° S
50° S

SCALE

0 — 500 — 1000 Kilometers

0 — 500 — 1000 Miles

Albers Equal–Area Projection

From *The Continents*, published by GoodYearBooks. Copyright © 1994 Jeanne and Arnold Cheyney.

Name _____ Date _____

WORD SEARCHING
DIRECTIONS

This grid contains hidden words. The hidden words appear in bold print in the list at the right. They can go up, down, across, at an angle, forward, or backward.

(air) **pollution** (a city problem)

airplanes (owned by wealthier station families)

(Australia is between Indian and South) **Pacific** (Oceans)

(Australia trades most with U.S. and) **Japan**

(Australian) **Alps**

Canberra (national capital)

(the climate is mostly warm and) **dry**

(the countryside is called the) **bush**

dams (store water for dry seasons)

emu (large, non-flying bird)

(Interior Australia is dry grassland or) **desert**

iron (ore)

(leading world producer of) **wool**

lift (Australian name for elevator)

(most people live along the) **coast**

(1976: national) **aid** (to Aborigines)

outback (name for interior Australia)

smallest (continent)

soccer (popular team sport)

(some coastal areas) **flood** (in wet season)

(sugar) **cane**

tea (favorite hot drink)

(Upper Australia, in the) **Tropics**

winter (season—May through October)

(world's largest) **coral** (reef—Great Barrier Reef)

A	G	L	J	N	D	P	A	C	I	F	I	C
N	P	S	A	B	H	M	Q	I	X	I	Y	S
F	U	P	W	U	O	R	B	D	R	T	E	D
A	A	L	P	S	K	W	O	O	L	C	B	O
J	I	V	F	H	E	I	N	K	Z	H	J	O
Y	R	D	C	M	E	N	A	C	S	I	R	L
G	P	O	L	L	U	T	I	O	N	W	T	F
O	L	N	Q	P	A	E	H	T	S	A	O	C
D	A	M	S	Z	T	R	O	P	I	C	S	A
G	N	C	K	D	T	J	B	U	L	X	H	N
V	E	M	A	F	R	S	Q	Z	W	R	A	B
O	S	P	I	S	E	E	O	D	B	U	M	E
T	U	L	D	E	S	Y	F	C	I	L	G	R
S	M	A	L	L	E	S	T	N	C	W	M	R
N	F	R	I	O	D	L	E	V	A	E	C	A
Y	R	O	P	X	S	V	A	Q	H	B	R	D
K	U	C	J	C	T	K	C	A	B	T	U	O

Sheep

STATES, MAINLAND TERRITORIES, AND CAPITALS

Name _____ Date _____

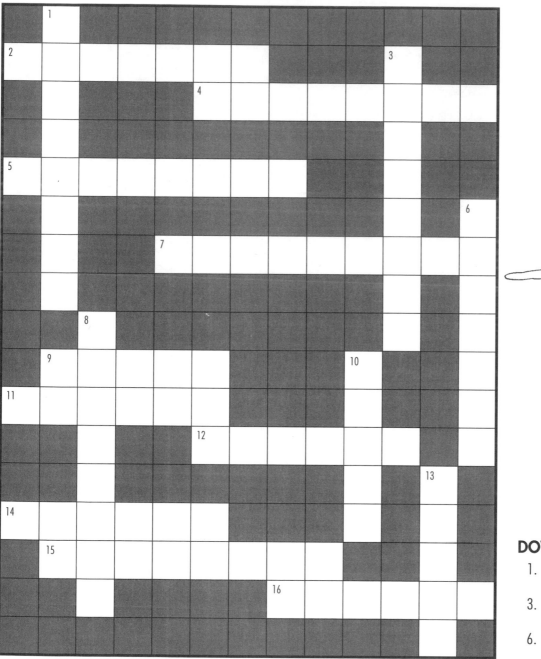

Kangaroo

Emu

CROSSWORD PUZZLE

ACROSS

2. Australian _____ Territory (within New South Wales); location of national capital
4. State capital of South Australia
5. National capital of Australia
7. Capital of Victoria
9. _____ Australia: the state south of Northern Territory
11. Capital of Northern Territory
12. Capital of Tasmania
14. The state east of Northern Territory: _____land
15. Capital of Queensland
16. Capital of New South Wales

DOWN

1. The state that is an island south of Australia
3. The state farthest south; north of Tasmania
6. The state west of South Australia; west of Northern Territory: _____ Australia
8. Territory north of South Australia: _____ Territory
10. Capital of Western Australia
13. The state south of Queensland: New South _____

From *The Continents*, published by GoodYearBooks. Copyright © 1994 Jeanne and Arnold Cheyney.

Name _____ Date _____

CROSSING OVER

DIRECTIONS

Use a pencil for this game. Find words from the following list (the words not in parentheses) that have the correct number of spaces and letters to fit into the crossing-over boxes. Each word has a place where it belongs. The first word is done for you. To continue, find a 4-letter word with a "t" in the third space, and so on. All the words tell about New Zealand.

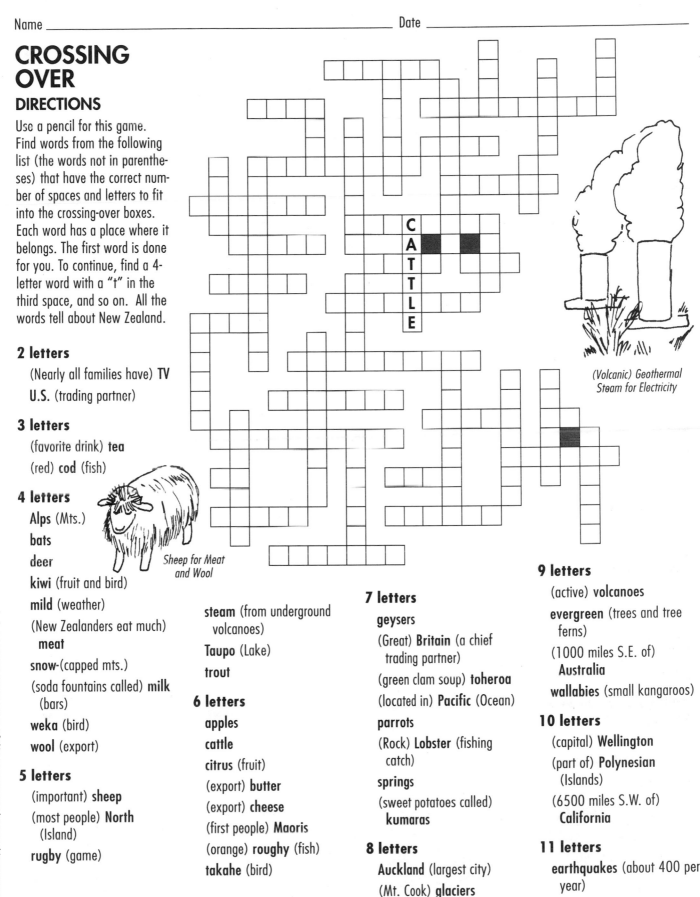

(Volcanic) Geothermal Steam for Electricity

Sheep for Meat and Wool

2 letters

(Nearly all families have) **TV**

U.S. (trading partner)

3 letters

(favorite drink) **tea**

(red) **cod** (fish)

4 letters

Alps (Mts.)

bats

deer

kiwi (fruit and bird)

mild (weather)

(New Zealanders eat much) **meat**

snow-(capped mts.)

(soda fountains called) **milk** (bars)

weka (bird)

wool (export)

5 letters

(important) **sheep**

(most people) **North** (Island)

rugby (game)

steam (from underground volcanoes)

Taupo (Lake)

trout

6 letters

apples

cattle

citrus (fruit)

(export) **butter**

(export) **cheese**

(first people) **Maoris**

(orange) **roughy** (fish)

takahe (bird)

7 letters

geysers

(Great) **Britain** (a chief trading partner)

(green clam soup) **toheroa**

(located in) **Pacific** (Ocean)

parrots

(Rock) **Lobster** (fishing catch)

springs

(sweet potatoes called) **kumaras**

8 letters

Auckland (largest city)

(Mt. Cook) **glaciers**

9 letters

(active) **volcanoes**

evergreen (trees and tree ferns)

(1000 miles S.E. of) **Australia**

wallabies (small kangaroos)

10 letters

(capital) **Wellington**

(part of) **Polynesian** (Islands)

(6500 miles S.W. of) **California**

11 letters

earthquakes (about 400 per year)

EUROPE

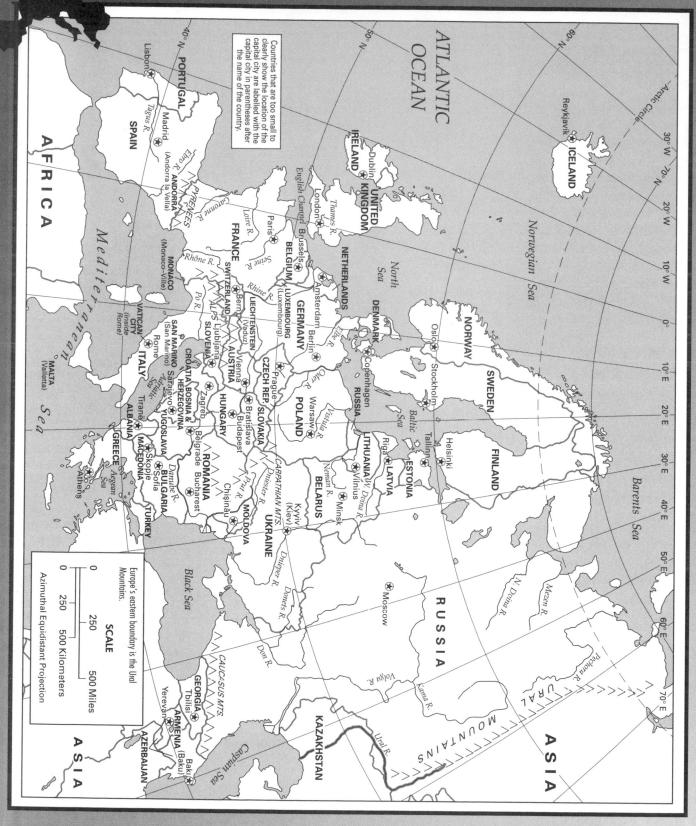

Countries that are too small to clearly show the location of the capital city are labelled with the capital city in parentheses after the name of the country.

Europe's eastern boundary is the Ural Mountains.

SCALE

Azimuthal Equidistant Projection

Name _____ Date _____

CROSSWORD PUZZLE

ACROSS

2. Largest European city
6. The Gulf Stream keeps most of Norway's coast _____ free.
7. Smallest country: _____ City
8. _____: important transportation routes
10. Europe handles over _____ of the world's shipping
11. A chief river
13. Very important grain crop
14. Four-lane superhighways in Germany: _____bahnen
15. The northern _____ is treeless and very cold.
18. Gulf Stream winds _____ Europe.
21. _____ Sea: world's largest lake (surrounded by land)
24. Initials for world's oldest airline (Netherlands)
25. Very important crop: _____ beets
26. Highest mountain in Europe: Mt. _____
27. A chief river (England)

DOWN

1. Over _____ languages are spoken.
3. Europe produces most of the world's _____.
4. Very important grain crop
5. Very important grain crop
8. One of the world's busiest ports: _____ (Netherlands)
9. Tidal power plant: gets its _____ power from incoming and outgoing tides.
12. Switzerland: world's largest motor-traffic _____
16. A chief river (Russia)
17. _____: cover the tundra in short, cold summers
18. Europe's chief grain crop
19. Longest European river
20. A chief French river
22. Chief mountain range
23. Over one-half of Europe is _____ land.

Germany

73

Name _____ Date _____

CROSSWORD PUZZLE

ACROSS

1. The country between Switzerland and Austria; on the Rhine R.
4. The country north of Spain; west of Italy, Switzerland, and Germany.
5. The country east of Germany; north of the Czech and the Slovak Republics
8. The country east of Finland
9. Great _____: the country surrounded by the North Sea and North Atlantic Ocean
10. The country north of Denmark; west of Sweden
14. The country north of Germany; south of Norway
15. The country northeast of France; south of the Netherlands
16. The country east of Sweden; bordering the Baltic Sea on the southern and western border
17. The country east of Norway; west of Finland
18. The country east of France; southwest of Germany; northwest of Italy

DOWN

1. The country southeast of Belgium; west of Germany; northeast of France
2. The island country in the North Atlantic Ocean; north of Ireland; west of Norway
3. The coastal country north of Belgium; west of Germany
6. The country north of Italy; west of Hungary
7. The _____ Republic: the country north of Austria; south of Poland
11. The country west of Great Britain; surrounded by the North Atlantic Ocean
12. The country west of Poland; east of the Netherlands
13. The _____ Republic: the country south of Poland; north of Hungary

Fishing

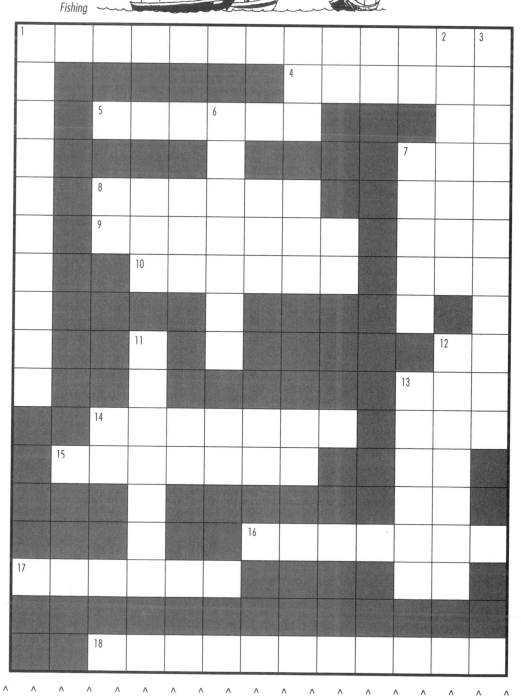

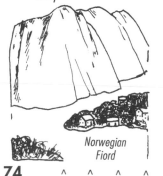

Norwegian Fiord

74

Name _____ Date _____

Berlin

Helsinki

CROSSWORD PUZZLE

ACROSS

1. Capital of Belgium
4. Capital of Austria
6. Capital of Germany
7. Capital of Russia
11. Capital of Switzerland
13. Capital of the Slovak Republic
15. Capital of Great Britain
17. Capital of Liechtenstein
18. Capital of Poland
19. Capital of the Netherlands

DOWN

2. Capital of Sweden
3. Capital of Finland
5. Capital of Denmark
8. Capital of Luxembourg
9. Capital of Ireland
10. Capital of the Czech Republic
12. Capital of Norway
14. Capital of Iceland
16. Capital of France

London

Name _____ Date _____

CROSSWORD PUZZLE

ACROSS

1. The country north of Bulgaria; east of Hungary
4. _____: (The European part of) the country southeast of Bulgaria; northeast of Greece
5. The country south of Romania; northeast of Greece
6. The country northwest of Greece; on the Adriatic Sea
8. The country in southern France; near the Italian border
10. The country southwest of France; bordering both the Mediterranean Sea and the North Atlantic Ocean
13. _____ City: a country on the western Italian coast; east of Corsica
14. The country south of Bulgaria and Albania; west of Turkey
15. The country bordering the North Atlantic Ocean; west of Spain

DOWN

2. The country south of Switzerland and Austria
3. The former country east of Italy; south of Hungary and Austria
7. The country in northeastern Spain; south of the French border
9. An island country in the Mediterranean Sea; south of Italy, east of Tunisia (Africa)
11. San _____: the country on the eastern Italian coast; east of Florence, Italy
12. The country west of Romania; east of Austria

Fishing

Outdoor Market

From *The Continents*, published by GoodYearBooks. Copyright © 1994 Jeanne and Arnold Cheyney.

SOUTHERN-AREA CAPITALS EUROPE

Name _____ Date _____

Andorra

Greece

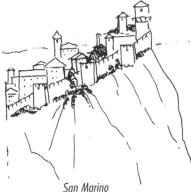

San Marino

CROSSWORD PUZZLE

ACROSS
3. Capital of Bulgaria
5. Capital of Romania
6. Capital of Malta
8. Capital of Spain
9. _____ Marino: capital of San Marino
12. Capital of Albania
13. Capital of Italy
14. Capital of Monaco

DOWN
1. Capital of Hungary
2. Capital of Serbia (former Yugoslavia)
4. Capital of Andorra
7. Capital of Turkey
10. Capital of Portugal
11. Capital of Greece

Albania

Malta

Name _____ Date _____

(FORMER SOVIET UNION) AND FOUR NON-MEMBERS CROSSWORD PUZZLE

ACROSS

1. The country southwest of Byelarus; partially surrounding Moldova
9. The country southeast of Uzbekistan; southwest of Kyrgyzstan
12. The country north and east of Lithuania; southwest of Estonia
13. The country north of Kazakhstan; east of Ukraine
14. The country south of Kazakhstan; northeast of Tadzhikistan

DOWN

1. The country east of Turkmenistan; west of Tadzhikistan
2. The country east of Armenia; southeast of Georgia
3. The country west of Azerbaijan; south of Georgia
4. The country west of Uzbekistan; bordering the Caspian Sea
5. The country northeast of Latvia; northwest of Russia
6. The country south of Lithuania; northeast of Ukraine
7. The country south of Russia; north of Uzbekistan
8. The country north of Byelarus; southwest of Latvia
10. The country north of Armenia; north of Azerbaijan
11. The country partially surrounded by Ukraine

Lithuania

From *The Continents*, published by GoodYearBooks. Copyright © 1994 Jeanne and Arnold Cheyney.

^ ^

Name _____ Date _____

(FORMER SOVIET UNION) AND FOUR NON-MEMBERS CROSSWORD PUZZLE

ACROSS

1. Capital of Latvia
2. Capital of Georgia
5. Capital of Uzbekistan
7. Capital of Kazakhstan: _____-Ata
9. Capital of Byelarus
10. Capital of Tadzhikistan
13. Capital of Moldova
14. Capital of Lithuania

DOWN

3. Capital of Azerbaijan
4. Capital of Turkmenistan
6. Capital of Estonia
8. Capital of Russia
11. Capital of Kyrgyzstan
12. Capital of Armenia
13. Capital of Ukraine

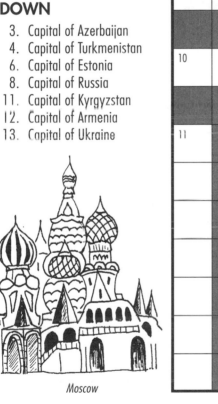

Moscow

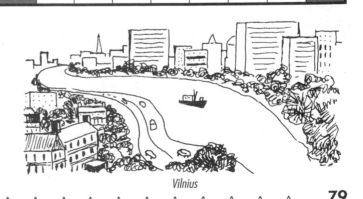

Riga

Vilnius

^ ^

Name _____ Date _____

N	E	T	R	A	M	C	B	E	G	R	E	T
D	L	E	B	R	M	L	E	M	M	I	N	G
G	K	H	E	L	C	H	A	M	O	I	S	O
A	I	T	I	B	B	A	R	N	X	P	S	H
F	T	K	J	O	O	N	I	B	O	R	T	E
O	W	L	R	A	T	Y	S	Q	F	R	O	G
U	E	D	V	R	E	I	N	D	E	E	R	D
F	L	O	W	C	P	I	J	W	A	B	K	E
Z	E	G	L	K	W	I	F	T	G	H	Y	H
Q	R	N	S	P	I	U	G	V	L	R	O	A
M	R	S	E	O	L	W	A	E	E	M	C	P
L	I	Z	A	R	D	Q	E	W	O	A	X	D
B	U	F	L	K	C	J	N	P	B	N	Z	H
G	Q	C	S	B	A	D	G	E	R	N	J	C
L	S	H	M	I	T	H	Y	G	O	F	M	N
I	E	D	R	W	O	R	R	A	P	S	K	I
N	I	G	H	T	I	N	G	A	L	E	L	F

Lemming

Eagle Owl

Stork

Brown Bear

WORD SEARCHING

DIRECTIONS

This grid contains hidden words. The hidden words appear in bold print in the list at the right. They can go up, down, across, at an angle, forward, or backward.

badger

(brown) **bear**

chamois (goat-like)

eagle

egret (bird)

elk

(eyed) **lizard**

finch

fox

frog

(ground) **squirrel**

hedgehog

(house) **sparrow**

nightingale (bird)

(Norway) **lemming**

otter

owl

(pine) **marten** (animal)

rabbit

reindeer

robin

seal

(white) **stork**

(wild) **boar**

wildcat

wolf

(wood) **pigeon**

Name _____ Date _____

SUPPLY THE VOWEL

DIRECTIONS

This grid contains hidden words. The hidden words appear in bold print in the list below. The words can go up, down, across, at angles, back-ward, or forward. Parts of words may overlap. Supply the correct vowel—
a e i o u—for the center of each word group.

- **barley**
- **chestnuts**
- **citrus** (fruits)
- **corn**
- **cotton**
- **dates**
- **figs**
- **flax**
- (flower) **bulbs**
- **grapes**
- **hemp**
- **hops**
- **oats**
- **olives**
- **potatoes**
- **rice**
- **sugar** (beets)
- **sunflower** (seeds)
- **tobacco**
- **wheat**

F	C	A	J	K	D	G	V	D	C	C	H	B
L	F	I	G	M	E	U	S	T	A	◯	I	E
B	N	L	R	D	P	W	A	J	P	T	R	S
T	O	B	◯	C	C	O	M	S	H	T	C	N
H	R	T	P	X	L	O	R	P	N	O	G	F
C	E	Q	E	W	S	S	B	V	T	N	A	Y
S	G	B	S	S	T	◯	N	T	S	E	H	C
T	I	J	F	M	L	N	G	L	Q	K	K	H
S	R	P	O	B	S	F	B	A	D	Z	T	U
E	D	O	S	Y	C	L	W	H	R	S	O	G
F	L	T	N	K	I	O	U	P	T	A	N	S
N	M	A	E	R	J	W	A	W	R	C	G	B
W	E	T	G	P	C	E	S	E	V	◯	L	O
I	H	O	M	O	M	R	L	U	F	T	C	Y
D	Y	◯	L	R	A	B	V	T	B	R	H	E
J	H	S	A	D	H	C	E	K	G	U	J	I
P	U	F	S	T	R	N	W	L	R	S	A	F

France

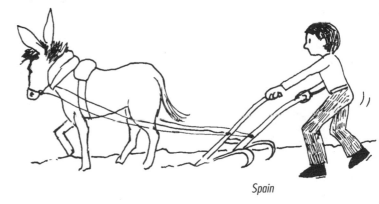

Spain

Name _____ Date _____

DIRECTIONS

All of the river names in the rectangle are written twice, except for one. Write the name of each river pair on a blank. (Cross off the pairs as you find them.) Then find the name of the river that appears only once and write it in the box.

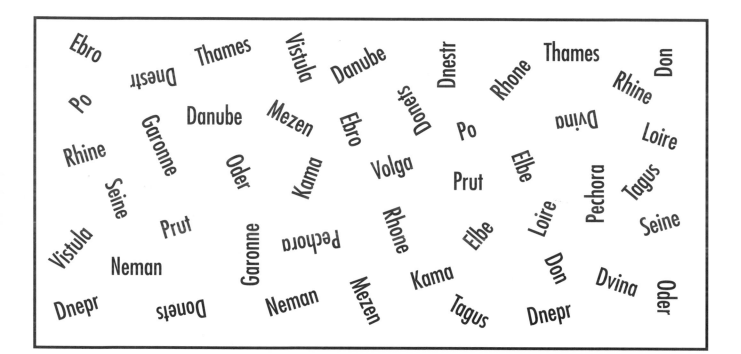

_____ _____ _____ _____

_____ _____ _____ _____

_____ _____ _____ _____

_____ _____ _____ _____

_____ _____ _____ _____

_____ _____ _____ _____

Castles on the Rhine River

Name _____ Date _____

NUMBER CODE
DIRECTIONS

Look at the number under each line. Find the matching number in the code box. Write the letter that matches that number on the corresponding answer lines.

A - 1	G - 7	M - 13	S - 19	Y - 25
B - 2	H - 8	N - 14	T - 20	Z - 26
C - 3	I - 9	O - 15	U - 21	
D - 4	J - 10	P - 16	V - 22	
E - 5	K - 11	Q - 17	W - 23	
F - 6	L - 12	R - 18	X - 24	

1. A sea north of Finland

1. ___ ___ ___ ___ ___ ___ ___
   2   1   18   5   14   20   19

2. A sea west of Norway

2. ___ ___ ___ ___ ___ ___ ___ ___ ___
   14   15   18   23   5   7   9   1   14

3. A sea north of Poland

3. ___ ___ ___ ___ ___ ___
   2   1   12   20   9   3

4. A sea west of Denmark

4. ___ ___ ___ ___ ___
   14   15   18   20   8

5. A large sea south of Europe

5. ___ ___ ___ ___ ___ ___ ___ ___ ___ ___ ___ ___ ___
   13   5   4   9   20   5   18   18   1   14   5   1   14

6. A sea north of Turkey

6. ___ ___ ___ ___ ___
   2   12   1   3   11

7. A sea east of Greece

7. ___ ___ ___ ___ ___ ___
   1   5   7   5   1   14

8. A sea east of Italy

8. ___ ___ ___ ___ ___ ___ ___ ___
   1   4   18   9   1   20   9   3

*City on a Rocky Island
in the Mediterranean Sea*

NAME THE POPULAR DISH

DIRECTIONS

Fill in the dotted lines with your answers. If they are correct, the circled letters will spell a popular dish in Austria.

1. Farm crop

2. Winter: world visitors come to the Alps to

3. Thick _____ cover much of the land.

4. Austria has no _____.

5. Chefs famous for _____ and pastry creations

6. Austria: for centuries a _____ center of Europe.

7. Health resorts

8. _____: homes with steep roofs hanging out over sides of houses

9. Unit of money

10. Austria is famous for its beautiful _____.

11. Sport: shoving heavy rock across the ice

12. The ruler is a _____.

13. Famous music composer of the 1700s

14. Important poultry product

15. Important mined mineral (seasoning)

Pastries

SCRAMBLED WORDS

DIRECTIONS

Unscramble the words and write the answers on the lines provided. (Use scrap paper to work out your answers.)

1. T S O A N I M U N cover 3/4 of Austria. _____

2. E N V A I N is the capital and largest city. _____

3. A chief income source for farmers is A R D I Y farming. _____

4. Most people speak R E G N A M. _____

5. An important crop is U R S G A S T E B E. _____

6. A chief income source for farmers: C L K S O I E V T _____

7. An important crop is O N C R. _____

Skiing

Name _____ Date _____

CROSSING OVER

DIRECTIONS

Use a pencil for this game. Find words from the following list (the words not in parentheses) that have the correct number of spaces and letters to fit into the crossing-over boxes. Each word has a place where it belongs. The first word is done for you. To continue, find a 7-letter word with "d" in the sixth space, and so on. All the words tell about Belgium.

4 letters

deer

flax

Genk (city)

hops (crop)

King (Head of State)

Leie (R.)

oats

(Van) Dyck (famous portrait painter)

5 letters

dairy (cattle)

(Flemings in the N.) Dutch (language)

Ghent (city)

Liége (city)

Meuse (R.)

North (Sea)

sugar (beets)

wheat

(wild) boars

6 letters

barley

(beef) cattle

Bruges (city)

(Walloons, in the S.) French (language)

7 letters

Antwerp (city)

Germany (E. border country)

(no) housing (shortage)

polders (lowlands)

(popular sport) bicycle (racing)

Schelde (R.)

8 letters

Brussels (capital)

Flemings (northern people)

(N. Belgium is called) Flanders

potatoes

Walloons (southern people)

wildcats

9 letters

(a favorite food) waterzooi (chowder)

10 letters

Luxembourg (a border country)

11 letters

Gendarmerie (police)

Netherlands (N. border country)

River Barge

Hand-made Lace

Barnyard

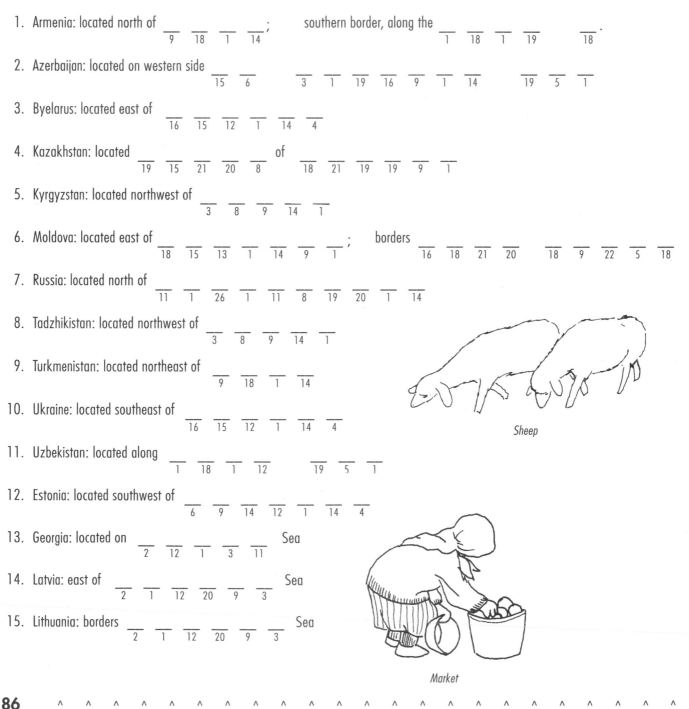

COMMONWEALTH OF INDEPENDENT STATES

^ ^

Name _____ Date _____

(FORMERLY U.S.S.R) NUMBER CODE

DIRECTIONS

Look at the number under each line. Find the matching number in the code box. Write the letter that matches that number on the corresponding answer lines.

A - 1	G - 7	M - 13	S - 19	Y - 25
B - 2	H - 8	N - 14	T - 20	Z - 26
C - 3	I - 9	O - 15	U - 21	
D - 4	J - 10	P - 16	V - 22	
E - 5	K - 11	Q - 17	W - 23	
F - 6	L - 12	R - 18	X - 24	

1. Armenia: located north of ___ ___ ___ ___ ; southern border, along the ___ ___ ___ ___ ___ .
   9 18 1 14   1 18 1 19 18

2. Azerbaijan: located on western side ___ ___ ___ ___ ___ ___ ___ ___ ___ ___ ___ ___
   15 6   3 1 19 16 9 1 14   19 5 1

3. Byelarus: located east of ___ ___ ___ ___ ___ ___
   16 15 12 1 14 4

4. Kazakhstan: located ___ ___ ___ ___ ___ of ___ ___ ___ ___ ___ ___
   19 15 21 20 8   18 21 19 19 9 1

5. Kyrgyzstan: located northwest of ___ ___ ___ ___ ___
   3 8 9 14 1

6. Moldova: located east of ___ ___ ___ ___ ___ ___ ___ ; borders ___ ___ ___ ___ ___ ___ ___ ___ ___
   18 15 13 1 14 9 1   16 18 21 20 18 9 22 5 18

7. Russia: located north of ___ ___ ___ ___ ___ ___ ___ ___ ___ ___
   11 1 26 1 11 8 19 20 1 14

8. Tadzhikistan: located northwest of ___ ___ ___ ___ ___
   3 8 9 14 1

9. Turkmenistan: located northeast of ___ ___ ___ ___
   9 18 1 14

10. Ukraine: located southeast of ___ ___ ___ ___ ___ ___
    16 15 12 1 14 4

11. Uzbekistan: located along ___ ___ ___ ___ ___ ___ ___
    1 18 1 12   19 5 1

12. Estonia: located southwest of ___ ___ ___ ___ ___ ___ ___
    6 9 14 12 1 14 4

13. Georgia: located on ___ ___ ___ ___ ___ Sea
    2 12 1 3 11

14. Latvia: east of ___ ___ ___ ___ ___ ___ Sea
    2 1 12 20 9 3

15. Lithuania: borders ___ ___ ___ ___ ___ ___ Sea
    2 1 12 20 9 3

Sheep

Market

^ ^

From *The Continents*, published by GoodYearBooks. Copyright © 1994 Jeanne and Arnold Cheyney.

Name _____ Date _____

RUSSIA SUPPLY THE VOWEL

DIRECTIONS

This grid contains hidden words. The hidden words appear in bold print in the list belwo.. The words can go up, down, across, at angles, backward, or forward. Parts of words may overlap. Supply the correct vowel—a e i o u—for the center of each word group.

icon (small religious painting)

(much) **forest** (area)

Gorki (a major city)

Moscow (capital)

(important crop) **wheat**

(North border) **Barents** (Sea)

(once ruled by) **Czars**

(St. Basil's church built by) **Ivan** (the Terrible)

(government encourages) **sports** (excellence)

(North) **reindeer** (raised)

winters (long and cold)

(crop) **potatoes**

B	D	J	G	C	Y	D	A	E	D	C	F	A
H	I	K	B	Z	N	B	F	S	W	R	Q	E
L	P	O	T	◯	T	O	E	S	◯	V	A	N
C	M	N	L	R	R	H	G	K	N	C	U	T
O	N	N	W	S	I	E	R	J	T	W	O	A
R	I	Q	P	V	K	O	N	V	E	Y	S	N
F	S	U	T	M	G	L	C	T	R	O	R	I
A	P	T	O	E	D	M	H	L	S	T	U	Q
F	R	A	N	G	K	J	N	I	T	O	P	B
G	R	◯	I	N	D	E	E	R	S	W	A	V
F	Y	H	A	S	B	H	Y	C	I	L	A	D
R	E	W	J	P	M	N	I	G	N	T	O	M
T	S	E	R	◯	F	I	D	J	◯	R	A	L
K	U	C	S	R	A	H	T	K	M	L	Q	P
T	A	C	W	T	U	T	R	S	M	G	F	R
D	O	N	V	S	S	O	S	Y	O	E	K	Z
W	C	O	M	T	V	R	F	B	C	Q	L	P

Cutting Bread

(Northern town) **Vorkuta**

(Russia was a) **communist** (country)

(important crop) **oats**

(important crop) **rye**

(one of world's largest countries in) **area**

(N.W. border country) **Finland**

(Eastern European border mountains) **Ural**

(N.W. border) **Gulf** (of Finland)

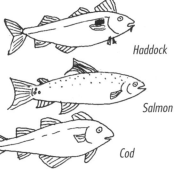

Haddock

Salmon

Cod

^ ^

Name _____   Date _____

C	H	K	F	S	E	L	S	T	B	S	Y	A
J	D	I	R	G	A	A	G	W	H	◯	A	T
D	N	A	L	◯	P	V	M	F	G	A	E	B
L	P	O	C	H	P	B	H	G	E	C	D	F
K	R	G	U	D	N	W	S	S	B	O	A	C
I	E	M	K	V	J	C	E	O	L	A	K	J
L	N	U	H	O	D	O	R	N	I	S	Q	K
S	F	G	G	R	T	S	M	T	M	T	R	N
E	N	P	R	◯	C	Y	A	S	A	A	O	P
B	D	E	T	K	R	V	E	B	◯	N	A	D
H	I	O	K	K	L	P	U	T	S	G	Q	V
J	P	F	G	C	M	T	R	C	T	P	A	T
D	U	M	P	L	◯	N	G	S	R	W	B	R
C	S	G	E	R	L	H	Q	P	I	S	U	W
E	A	I	O	U	K	T	C	J	A	D	E	A
K	O	N	M	H	I	B	K	H	O	F	L	Y
Y	L	V	D	G	F	J	N	T	P	R	M	C

Prague

SUPPLY THE VOWEL

DIRECTIONS

This grid contains hidden words. The hidden words appear in bold print in the list at the right. The words can go up, down, across, at angles, backward, or forward. Parts of words may overlap. Supply the correct vowel—a e i o u—for the center of each word group.

Austria (to the south)

beef

chickens

coal

Danube (River)

dumplings (dough in broth)

Dvořák (famous composer)

eggs

(fish) **carp** (Christmas dish)

hogs

iron (ore)

milk

(no) **seacoast**

Poland (to the north)

pork (a favorite)

potatoes

Prague (capital of the Czech Republic)

(sauer)**kraut** (a favorite)

sugar (beets)

wheat

^ ^

Name _____ Date _____

WORD SEARCHING

DIRECTIONS

This grid contains hidden words. The hidden words appear in bold print in the list below. They can go up, down, across, at an angle, forward, or backward.

Farm

bacon

barley (world producer)

butter

cheese (export)

Copenhagen (capital)

(famous) **Danish** (pastries)

(famous) **porcelain** (figurines)

(Hans Christian) **Andersen** (fairy tales)

Kringle (nut-filled coffee cake)

(nearly surrounded by) **water**

(people eat four) **meals** (a day)

smorrebrod (favorite sandwich)

soccer (favorite sport)

(statue of Little) **Mermaid**

storks (build nests on roofs)

(stuffed) **duckling** (a favorite food)

(3/4) **farm** (land)

Tivoli (famous amusement park)

Little Mermaid Copenhagen

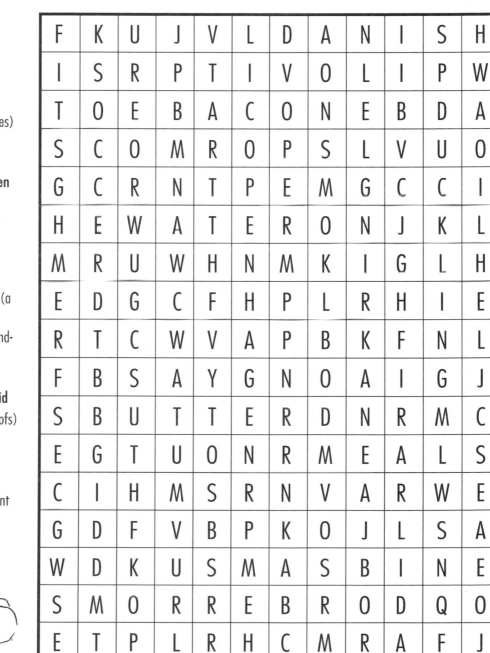

F	K	U	J	V	L	D	A	N	I	S	H	P
I	S	R	P	T	I	V	O	L	I	P	W	O
T	O	E	B	A	C	O	N	E	B	D	A	R
S	C	O	M	R	O	P	S	L	V	U	O	C
G	C	R	N	T	P	E	M	G	C	C	I	E
H	E	W	A	T	E	R	O	N	J	K	L	L
M	R	U	W	H	N	M	K	I	G	L	H	A
E	D	G	C	F	H	P	L	R	H	I	E	I
R	T	C	W	V	A	P	B	K	F	N	L	N
F	B	S	A	Y	G	N	O	A	I	G	J	D
S	B	U	T	T	E	R	D	N	R	M	C	L
E	G	T	U	O	N	R	M	E	A	L	S	B
C	I	H	M	S	R	N	V	A	R	W	E	K
G	D	F	V	B	P	K	O	J	L	S	A	Y
W	D	K	U	S	M	A	S	B	I	N	E	Y
S	M	O	R	R	E	B	R	O	D	Q	O	N
E	T	P	L	R	H	C	M	R	A	F	J	A

Name _____ Date _____

NAME A CHIEF INDUSTRY
DIRECTIONS

Fill in the dotted lines with your answers. If they are correct, the circled letters will spell a chief industry in Finland.

Glassware

1. A crop of southern Finland 1. ◯ _ _ _ _
2. Finland is known as the "Land of _____ of lakes." 2. _ _ ◯ _ _ _ _ _ _
3. Most people live in _____ Finland. 3. _ ◯ _ _ _ _ _
4. Northern Finland is part of "The Land of the _____ Sun." 4. _ _ ◯ _ _ _ _ _ _ _
5. (A chief industry) making 5. ◯ _ _ _ _ _ _
6. Most valuable natural resource 6. _ ◯ _ _ _ _
7. Northern area: frozen, treeless plain 7. _ _ _ _ ◯ _
8. Capital 8. _ _ _ _ _ _ _ ◯ _
9. Finland is famous for building these ships 9. ◯ _ _ _ _ _ _ _ _ _ _
10. The Finns have a special bath called a 10. _ _ _ ◯ _
11. A crop 11. _ _ ◯ _ _ _ _ _

FINLAND SKYSCRAPER
DIRECTIONS

Write your answers in the boxes. The circled letters will help you.

1. A chief crop
2. A chief crop
3. Important forest tree
4. A favorite food (sea)
5. A poultry product
6. A chief crop
7. A favorite food: boiled potatoes covered with _____ and dill.
8. Western border country
9. A river
10. A special meat treat: smoked _____
11. Important manufactured product
12. Important manufactured product (sets)

Reindeer

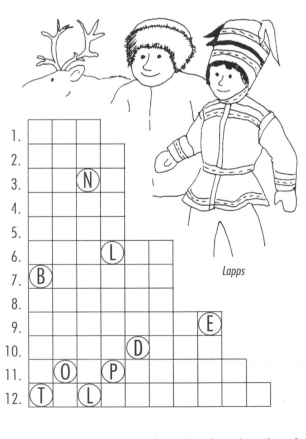

Lapps

1.
2.
3. ◯N
4.
5.
6. ◯L
7. ◯B
8.
9. ◯E
10. ◯D
11. ◯O ◯P
12. ◯T ◯L

Name _____ Date _____

CROSSWORD PUZZLE

ACROSS

1. An edible snail
5. Longest river
7. Fishing catch
8. A vegetable crop
9. Tour de France: (_____ race) greatest national sports event
14. Farm animal
15. _____ Bonaparte: conquered much of Europe (1700s and 1800s).
16. Castles are called _____.
20. Independence (1792): _____ Day
22. Paris: a great _____ center.
24. Famous stone arch in Paris: Arc de _____
25. A river

DOWN

1. Famous Paris tower
2. French _____ (mountains)
3. Unit of money
4. Vacation center on the Mediterranean Sea
6. Fishing catch
10. A city
11. A crop: _____flower seeds
12. A chief grain crop
13. A tree: cork _____
17. France is the _____ western European country.
18. Capital
19. A fruit crop
21. Famous cathedral: Notre _____
23. A grain crop

Artist

Arc de Triomphe

Eiffel Tower

Name _____ Date _____

CROSSWORD PUZZLE

ACROSS

1. A famous composer
3. An important river
4. An important river
5. A chief grain crop
6. Mountain Range: Bavarian _____
7. A chief grain crop
9. A southern city
10. 1990: East and West Germany were _____
12. _____ Forest: picturesque old villages
13. A chief grain crop
14. Most popular sport
20. A chief vegetable crop
23. Important farm animals

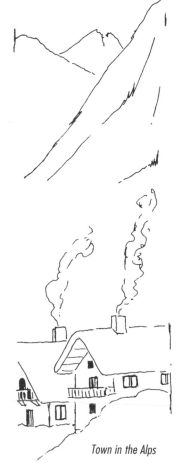

Town in the Alps

DOWN

1. Capital
2. A famous composer
8. A defeated World War II leader
11. A farm animal that provides 2/3 of the meat produced for food
14. A chief crop: _____ beets
15. A chief grain crop
16. Ancient _____ still stand along the Rhine River.
17. Important mined mineral
18. Important: _____ cattle
19. Important farm animals
21. Important farm animals
22. A river

From *The Continents*, published by GoodYearBooks. Copyright © 1994 Jeanne and Arnold Cheyney.

Castle Along the Rhine River

GREAT BRITAIN EUROPE

(ENGLAND AND WALES) CROSSWORD PUZZLE

ACROSS

1. England: trucks are called _____.
5. Popular Welsh food: cheese _____ (butter, cheese melted on toast)
7. The law-making body in England
9. Fish catch
11. Workers _____ petroleum and natural gas from the North Sea.
12. Fields are edged with _____ and hedges.
13. Important mined mineral
14. A farm animal
16. Great Britain was once the largest world _____ in history.
17. England: famous for double-decker _____.
18. A favorite place to socialize
19. England: gasoline is called _____.
20. Great Britain: ruler is a king or _____
21. Wales: favorite sport
23. Welsh mountains
24. Wales: world famous for male _____.

8. A great _____ nation (with many factories)
10. Important dairy product
15. England: most important farm animal

18. English unit of money
22. A marsh is called a _____

Tower of London

DOWN

1. England: the _____ country in Great Britain.
2. England: a dessert is called a _____
3. _____: a poultry product
4. A river in Wales and England
6. Important field crop for animals
7. Important vegetable crop

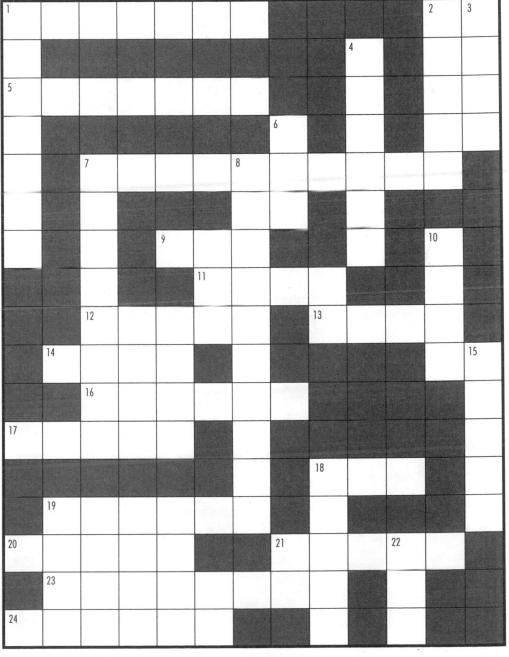

From *The Continents*, published by GoodYearBooks. Copyright © 1994 Jeanne and Arnold Cheyney.

Name _____ Date _____

(SCOTLAND AND NORTHERN IRELAND) CROSSWORD PUZZLE

ACROSS

1. A Scotland field crop
4. Scotland: a famous ancient hilltop fortress in the capital city: Edinburgh _____
5. Robert Louis Stevenson, a Scot, wrote _____ *Island* and *Kidnapped*.
7. Scotland: Loch Ness is famous for its _____.
8. Most land is _____land.
10. Scot landowners are called _____.
11. Northern Ireland: many homes are heated with _____, a fuel people dig from the ground.
12. Northern Ireland: a place where people socialize
13. A famous play, Peter _____, was written by a Scot, James Barrie.
17. A Scottish word for lakes
19. Scotland has _____faced sheep that can survive the cold winters.
20. A fruit tree
21. Northern Ireland: famous for its Irish _____ (cloth)
22. Northern Ireland: important vegetable crop
23. Northern Ireland: important field crop
24. Important farm animal
25. An article of Scottish clothing

26. Northern Ireland: fields are _____
27. Scotland: a favorite sport
28. Northern Ireland is often called _____.

DOWN

1. Ireland builds _____.
2. Ireland beverage

3. Scottish farmers are called _____.
6. Each Scottish clan has a plaid design called a _____.
9. Northern Ireland builds warships and ocean _____.
11. A fruit tree

14. Scotland: famous for things made from _____
15. Scotland: covered with _____
16. A famous Scottish musical instrument
18. Families with the same name and ancestry are called _____.

^ ^

Name _____ Date _____

NUMBER CODE
DIRECTIONS

Look at the number under each line. Find the matching number in the code box. Write the letter that matches that number on the corresponding answer lines.

A - 1	G - 7	M - 13	S - 19	Y - 25
B - 2	H - 8	N - 14	T - 20	Z - 26
C - 3	I - 9	O - 15	U - 21	
D - 4	J - 10	P - 16	V - 22	
E - 5	K - 11	Q - 17	W - 23	
F - 6	L - 12	R - 18	X - 24	

1. Capital and largest city: ___ ___ ___ ___ ___ ___
                                           1 20 8 5 14 19

2. One-fifth of Greece is ___ ___ ___ ___ ___ ___ ___ .
                                   9 19 12 1 14 4 19

3. Greece has one of the world's ___ ___ ___ ___ ___ ___ ___ ___ ___ ___ ___ ___ ___ ___
                                       12 1 18 7 5 19 20   13 5 18 3 8 1 14 20

   ___ ___ ___ ___ ___ ___ .
   6 12 5 5 20 19

4. The first two letters of the Greek alphabet: ___ ___ ___ ___ ___ and ___ ___ ___ ___ ,
                                                        1 12 16 8 1   2 5 20 1

   the words from which the word ___ ___ ___ ___ ___ ___ ___ ___ comes.
                                        1 12 16 8 1 2 5 20

5. The first ___ ___ ___ ___ ___ ___ ___ ___ ___ ___ ___ ___ ___ ___ ___ ___
                       15 12 25 13 16 9 3   7 1 13 5 19   23 5 18 5

   ___ ___ ___ ___ ___ ___ ___ ___ ___ ___ ___ ___ .
   8 5 12 4   9 14   7 18 5 5 3 5

6. ___ ___ ___ ___ ___ ___ ___ ___ ___ ___ ___ ___ ___ ___ ___ ___ ___ ___
   13 15 21 14 20 1 9 14 19   3 15 22 5 18   13 15 19 20

   ___ ___ ___ ___ ___ ___ ___ ___ .
   15 6   7 18 5 5 3 5

7. A leading world-producer of ___ ___ ___ ___ ___ ___ , ___ ___ ___ ___ ___ ___ , and
                                      12 5 13 15 14 19   15 12 9 22 5 19

   ___ ___ ___ ___ ___ ___ ___ .
   18 1 9 19 9 14 19

8. Famous Greek musical instruments: ___ ___ ___ ___ ___ ___ ___ ___ ___
                                     2 15 21 26 15 21 11 9 19

9. The famous ___ ___ ___ ___ ___ ___ ___ ___ ___ was built in around 400 B.C.
                   16 1 18 20 8 5 14 15 14

10. Favorite meeting places: ___ ___ ___ ___ ___ ___ ___ ___ ___ ___ ___ ___
                             3 15 6 6 5 5   8 15 21 19 5 19

11. Favorite meat: ___ ___ ___ ___
                  12 1 13 2

12. Greeks cook in ___ ___ ___ ___ ___ ___ ___ ___ .
                     15 12 9 22 5   15 9 12

13. Favorite food: ___ ___ ___ ___ ___ ___ ___ ___ ___ (ground meat and eggplant)
                  13 15 21 19 19 1 11 1

Goats

Making Thread

Folk Costume

Bouzouki

^ ^

Name _____ Date _____

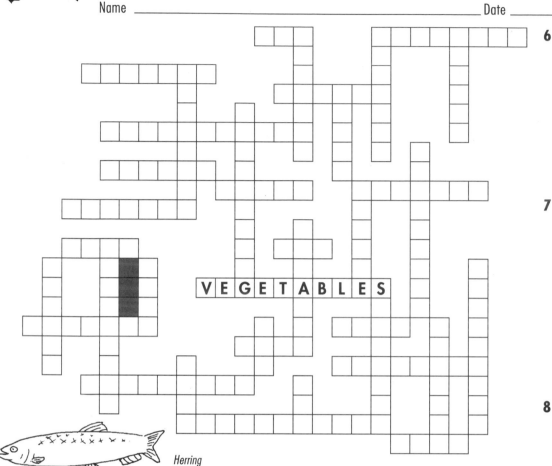

V E G E T A B L E S

Herring

CROSSING OVER

DIRECTIONS

Use a pencil for this game. Find words from the following list (the words not in parentheses) that have the correct number of spaces and letters to fit into the crossing-over boxes. Each word has a place where it belongs. The first word is done for you. To continue, find a 7-letter word with "a" in the fourth space, and so on. All the words tell about Iceland.

Greenhouse for Winter Vegetables

6 letters

cattle (raised)

(Gulf) **Stream** (warms much of the coast)

horses (raised)

(Iceland below) **Arctic** (circle)

(Iceland is an) **island**

7 letters

bananas (greenhouses)

capelin (fish catch)

Denmark (once ruled)

flowers (greenhouses)

herring (fish catch)

(some) geysers

Thjórsá (longest R.)

turnips (summer vegetable)

8 letters

(book) **printing** (many jobs)

glaciers (ice sheets)

tomatoes (greenhouses)

(winter) **swimming** (indoors)

9 letters

Icelandic (spoken language)

(living) expensive

(over 200) volcanoes (erupted)

Reykjavík (capital)

10 letters

publishing (many jobs)

vegetables (greenhouses)

11 letters

bookbinding (many jobs)

greenhouses (near hot springs)

3 letters

cod (fish catch)

hay (a chief crop)

(June) sun (nearly 24 hours daily)

(many) hot (springs)

4 letters

(December) dark (nearly 24 hours daily)

fish (a favorite food)

(hot) dogs (made with lamb)

lamb (a favorite meat)

(much) rain (summer)

(1700s) lava (destroyed farms; many people starved)

5 letters

(hot springs water) piped (to houses)

sheep (raised)

From *The Continents*, published by GoodYearBooks. Copyright © 1994 Jeanne and Arnold Cheyney.

Name _____ Date _____

WHAT IS IRELAND SOMETIMES CALLED?
DIRECTIONS

Fill in the dotted lines with your answers. If they are correct, the circled letters will spell what Ireland is sometimes called.

1. 1840s: a potato _____ killed thousands of people.
2. _____ land covers 2/3 of Ireland.
3. Much of Ireland is covered with _____ bogs.
4. Saint _____ brought Christianity to Ireland.
5. A chief food (vegetable)
6. Capital
7. A chief food (grain) product

8. Famous stone art work: _____ crosses
9. Longest river in the British Isles
10. Irish like _____ music.
11. _____ Britain once ruled.

1. _ _ _ _ _ ◯
2. _ _ _ ◯
3. _ ◯ _ _ _
4. _ _ _ _ ◯ _ _ _
5. _ _ _ _ ◯ _ _ _ _
6. _ _ _ ◯ _ _
7. _ _ _ _ ◯
8. _ _ _ _ ◯ _
9. ◯ _ _ _ _ _
10. _ _ _ ◯
11. _ _ ◯ _ _

Celtic Cross

IRELAND SKYSCRAPER
DIRECTIONS

Write your answers in the boxes. The circled letters will help you.

1. People gather here to socialize (a place).
2. A chief fishing catch
3. Field crop that's fed to cattle
4. Famous dish: Irish _____
5. A river
6. A dairy product
7. Important farm animal
8. Most farmland is used for _____ for animals.
9. A poultry animal
10. _____ is not legal in Ireland (dissolving a marriage).
11. A chief fishing catch
12. The harp: a favorite musical _____

Gathering Potatoes

Farm

From *The Continents*, published by GoodYearBooks. Copyright © 1994 Jeanne and Arnold Cheyney.

^ ^

Name _____ Date _____

WORD SEARCHING

DIRECTIONS

This grid contains hidden words. The hidden words appear in bold print in the list below. They can go up, down, across, at an angle, forward, or backward.

(Alps: good) **skiing**

Genoa (important port)

lemons (crop)

(melting snow provides) **electricity**

Michelangelo (famous artist)

Northern (Italy: industrialized and more prosperous)

olives (a world producer)

opera (a favorite entertainment)

pasta (flour and water dough)

Po (farm valley and a river)

rice

Rome (capital)

(1300s) **Renaissance** (time in history)

Vatican (City: center for Catholic church)

Venice (some streets: canals)

wheat (a chief crop)

wine (world producer)

C	G	M	I	A	L	R	F	S	V	P	J	K
E	L	E	C	T	R	I	C	I	T	Y	A	R
B	R	L	N	D	E	C	O	Y	T	O	C	W
O	P	E	R	A	L	E	A	F	N	L	G	I
B	H	M	N	O	K	W	T	E	J	E	I	N
V	R	O	S	A	U	B	G	E	W	G	D	E
M	C	N	S	K	I	I	N	G	D	N	A	Y
H	I	S	K	N	G	S	W	H	E	A	T	F
H	Q	L	P	J	T	U	S	S	P	L	E	N
O	B	V	E	N	I	C	E	A	C	E	Y	R
N	E	M	H	G	K	F	V	L	N	H	D	E
A	W	O	S	P	O	T	R	R	U	C	M	H
C	D	N	I	A	E	I	C	O	V	I	E	T
I	R	J	Q	S	J	P	H	M	G	M	U	R
T	K	M	O	T	N	S	S	E	V	I	L	O
A	R	N	A	A	Y	W	C	G	F	T	M	N
V	Y	A	I	K	B	H	L	P	B	D	A	V

Resort

^ ^

Name _____ Date _____

24. Very important dairy product
25. Electric _____ draw water out of drained land.
26. Name for wooden shoes

DOWN
1. The Netherlands are often called _____.
3. Mineral: natural _____
4. Important dairy product
5. The _____ Zee, once a bay, was diked in, drained, and is now 710 square miles of land.
9. The Netherlands are famous for this flower
13. A fishing catch
14. An important vehicle for transportation
15. A field crop
16. A fair is called a _____.
18. A mined mineral (seasoning)
19. _____ hold back the sea.
21. Climate: cool and _____
23. Initials for the Royal Dutch Airlines

CROSSWORD PUZZLE

ACROSS

2. Very important occupation
6. A drained area is a _____.
7. Important horticultural crop
8. Capital
10. Nearly half the land was once under _____.
11. Canals drain water from the _____.
12. December 5: gifts are exchanged on St. _____ Eve.
16. The ruler is a _____ or queen.
17. _____ Sea storms cause floods and dike leaks.
20. _____ products (most important foods)
22. Winter: people _____ on the canals.

Amsterdam

Name _____ Date _____

NAME THE FAVORITE SANDWICH SPREAD
DIRECTIONS

Fill in the dotted lines with your answers. If they are correct, the circled letters will spell Norway's favorite sandwich spread.

1. Norway: sometimes called "The Land of the _____ Sun"

2. Long inlets along the coast are called _____.

3. People eat four or five _____ a day.

4. Norway has one of the world's largest fishing and shipping _____.

5. Most children learn to ski before they start _____.

6. An important fish catch

7. Rushing rivers make cheap _____ power.

8. A chief mineral export

9. The national sport

10. The Gulf Stream keeps most seaports _____.

Farmland

Oslo

NORWAY SKYSCRAPER
DIRECTIONS

Write your answers in the boxes. The circled letters will help you.

1. A chief crop for cattle

2. The head of Norway is the _____ or queen.

3. Norway's capital

4. As early as the 1200s, dried _____ was exported (sea catch).

5. Far-northern people

6. The northern third of Norway is above the _____ Circle.

7. At one time, _____ lived in Norway, Sweden, and Finland.

8. The person with power is the prime _____ .

9. Some farmers raise _____ (animals).

10. An official appointed by the legislature who listens to complaints about the government.

11. Norway, Sweden, and Denmark are called _____ countries.

Farm by a Fiord

Village

100

From *The Continents*, published by GoodYearBooks. Copyright © 1994 Jeanne and Arnold Cheyney.

Name _____   Date _____

CROSSING OVER

DIRECTIONS

Use a pencil for this game. Find words from the following list (the words not in parentheses) that have the correct number of spaces and letters to fit into the crossing-over boxes. Each word has a place where it belongs. The first word is done for you. To continue, find a 7-letter word with "d" in the sixth space, and so on. All the words tell about Spain.

3 letters
cod (fish catch)

4 letters
beef
goat (popular meat)
lamb (popular meat)
tuna (a chief product)

5 letters
(climate) **sunny**
paseo (a walk before the evening meal)
sheep (chief livestock)
sugar (beets)
wheat
(a world leader) **olive** (crop)

6 letters
barley (a chief crop)
France (north border)
lemons
Madrid (capital)
paella (popular dish)
rabbit (popular meat)
siesta (afternoon nap)
soccer (popular sport)

7 letters
Basques (people in northwest Spain)
(Don) **Quixote** (written by Cervantes)
fishing (a chief occupation)
oranges

8 letters
alcazars (fortified castles)
(Christopher) **Columbus** (sailed from Spain)
flamenco (favorite dance)
(north border) **Pyrenees** (Mts.)
tomatoes

9 letters
(language) **Castilian** (Spanish)

10 letters
bullfights (popular)

11 letters
(many rural homes) **whitewashed**
(a world leader) **automobiles**

13 letters
(east coast) **Mediterranean** (Sea)

Alcasár

Gathering Olives

Traditional Costume

Shepherd in Goatskin

S U G A R

Name _____ Date _____

WORD SEARCHING

DIRECTIONS

This grid contains hidden words. The hidden words appear in bold print in the list below.. They can go up, down, across, at an angle, forward, or backward.

Town

S	A	D	F	R	E	E	D	N	I	E	R	P
T	S	G	I	C	H	M	A	K	B	J	C	O
O	C	E	P	G	N	I	I	K	S	I	Q	T
C	I	O	L	U	O	T	R	S	T	A	O	A
K	T	B	W	Y	R	S	Y	C	S	V	R	T
H	S	C	F	H	W	E	R	D	E	A	K	O
O	A	K	I	G	A	A	O	P	R	R	L	E
L	N	M	R	O	Y	A	T	V	O	N	I	S
M	M	G	J	T	B	D	S	P	F	A	R	M
L	Y	W	H	E	A	T	Y	E	K	C	O	H
F	G	U	K	B	E	E	F	C	H	E	N	I
M	O	S	M	O	R	G	A	S	B	O	R	D
J	Y	E	L	R	A	B	B	D	V	Y	N	R
S	P	A	E	G	G	U	K	G	Q	T	H	L
W	J	P	G	R	U	N	D	S	K	O	L	A
O	A	I	E	R	S	W	U	P	F	Y	M	C
P	N	A	L	A	I	R	T	S	U	D	N	I

(all children) **gymnastics** (in school)

barley

(a chief sport) **hockey** (ice)

(a chief sport) **skiing**

farm (land, in the south)

forests (more than 1/2 of Sweden)

Göteborg (shipbuilding center)

iron (ore, chief mineral)

(a leading) **paper** (producer)

(much farm income) **dairy** (cattle)

(much farm income) **beef** (cattle)

(north) **reindeer** (Lapp people)

oats

pork

potatoes

(primary school) **grundskola**

(prosperous) **industrial** (nation)

smörgasbord (many foods on a table)

Stockholm (capital)

sugar (beets)

(upper Sweden) **Arctic** (Circle)

(west border country) **Norway**

wheat

Name _____ Date _____

NUMBER CODE
DIRECTIONS

Look at the number under each line. Find the matching number in the code box. Write the letter on the that matches that number corresponding answer lines.

A - 1	G - 7	M - 13	S - 19	Y - 25
B - 2	H - 8	N - 14	T - 20	Z - 26
C - 3	I - 9	O - 15	U - 21	
D - 4	J - 10	P - 16	V - 22	
E - 5	K - 11	Q - 17	W - 23	
F - 6	L - 12	R - 18	X - 24	

1. Famous for __ __ __ __ __ __ __ , __ __ __ __ __ __ and
   23 1 20 3 8 5 19   3 8 5 5 19 5

   __ __ __ __ __ __ __ __ __ __
   3 8 15 3 15 12 1 20 5 19

2. A chief industry: __ __ __ __ __ __ __
   2 1 14 11 9 14 7

3. Capital: __ __ __ __
   2 5 18 14

4. Largest city: __ __ __ __ __ __
   26 21 18 9 3 8

5. Switzerland has remained __ __ __ __ __ __ __ __ __ __ __ __ __ __ __ __ __ __
   14 5 21 20 18 1 12   9 14   5 21 18 15 16 5 1 14

   __ __ __ __ , but it maintains a __ __ __ __ __ __ __ , __ __ __ __
   23 1 18 19   3 9 20 26 5 14 19   1 18 13 25

   called a __ __ __ __ __ __ __ , and all men, beginning at age 20, must __ __ __ __
   13 9 12 9 20 9 1   20 1 11 5

   __ __ __ __ __ __ __ .
   20 18 1 9 14 9 14 /

6. Swiss authors: __ __ __ __ __ __ __ __ __ __ __ __ __ __ __ __
   10 15 8 1 14 14 1   19 16 25 18 9   23 18 15 20 5

   __ __ __ __ __ ; the __ __ __ __ __ __ __ __ __ __ __ __ __ __ __
   8 5 9 4 9   23 25 19 19   6 1 13 9 12 25   23 18 15 20 5

   the __ __ __ __ __ __ __ __ __ __ __ __ __ __ __ __ __ __ __
   19 23 9 19 19   6 1 13 9 12 25   18 15 2 9 14 19 15 14

7. Famous mountains: __ __ __ __ __ __ __ __ __
   19 23 9 19 19   1 12 16 19

8. Famous high mountain peak: __ __ __ __ __ __ __ __ __ __ __ , on the south
   13 1 20 20 5 18 8 15 18 14

   __ __ __ __ __ __
   2 15 18 4 5 18

9. Some Swiss sports: __ __ __ __ __ __ , __ __ __ __ __ __ __ __
   19 11 9 9 14 7   3 12 9 13 2 9 14 7

   __ __ __ __ __ __ __ __ __ __ , __ __ __ __ __ __
   2 15 2 19 12 5 4 4 9 14 7   8 9 11 9 14 7

   __ __ __ __ __ __ __ __
   2 9 3 25 3 12 9 14 7

Resort Town

Mountain Village

NORTH AMERICA

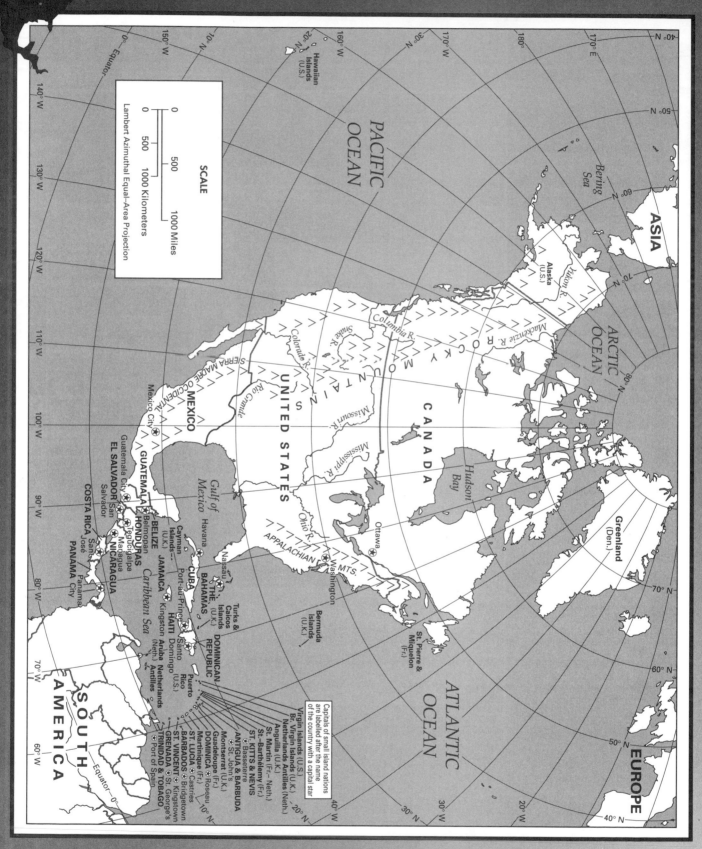

From *The Continents*, published by GoodYearBooks. Copyright © 1994 Jeanne and Arnold Cheyney.

Name _____ Date _____

Rockies

26. Important grain crop for cattle
27. Cold-North animal: _____ bear
28. Largest western tree
29. One of the Great Lakes

DOWN

2. World's largest fresh-water lake (one of the 5 Great Lakes)
3. North America is the _____-largest continent.
4. World-famous falls
5. The Caribbean Islands are called the West _____.
8. Large forest animal: black _____
11. Canada and U.S. export more _____ than any other world region.
13. Eastern border: Atlantic _____.
14. North America is covered with much good _____ land.
15. S.W. desert: _____ cactus
20. Small S.W. desert animals
21. Important farm animals: beef _____

CROSSWORD PUZZLE

ACROSS

1. Most U. S. deserts are in the South-_____ area.
6. The largest Caribbean island
7. Southern U.S. tree
9. World's largest island
10. Western tree
12. Cold North bird: snowy _____
14. _____ cover much of North America.
16. Important grain crop for humans
17. Capital of U.S.: Washington, _____
18. North border ocean
19. Highest N. American mt.
21. A Great Plains wild animal
22. Central Greenland is covered with an _____ cap that never thaws.
23. Smaller animal found throughout N. America
24. Dangerous snake: _____ snake
25. Most important grain crop

Name _____ Date _____

CROSSWORD PUZZLE

ACROSS

1. St. _____ (called St. Kitts) & Nevis: islands west of Antigua
4. The country north of the United States
5. St. _____ & the Grenadines—island north of Trinidad; south of St. Lucia
7. An island north of Tobago; east of St. Vincent
11. _____ & Barbuda; island east and northeast of St. Christopher (St. Kitts) and Nevis
14. The country north of Costa Rica; south of Honduras
18. The country connecting South America to Central America
19. The island northwest of Tobago; south of St. Vincent
20. An island north of the island of Martinique; south of Guadeloupe
22. The country west of Honduras; west of Belize; south of Mexico

DOWN

2. The country southeast of Cuba; west of Dominican Republic
3. The country north of Nicaragua; east of Guatemala
4. The country northwest of Haiti; north of Jamaica
6. Dominican _____: the country east of Haiti; west of Puerto Rico
8. El _____: the country bordering the Pacific Ocean; southwest of Guatemala
9. St. _____: island north of St. Vincent; northwest of Barbados
10. _____ & Tobago: islands close to Venezuela, South America
12. The islands closest to southeastern Florida, U.S.A.
13. Costa _____: the country northwest of Panama; south of Nicaragua
15. The island south of Cuba; southwest of Haiti
16. The country that borders the southwestern United States
17. The country bordering the Caribbean Sea; northeast of Guatemala
21. The country south of Canada; north of Mexico

Beach

From *The Continents*, published by GoodYearBooks. Copyright © 1994 Jeanne and Arnold Cheyney.

CAPITALS OF INDEPENDENT COUNTRIES NORTH AMERICA

^ ^

Name _____ Date _____

CROSSWORD PUZZLE

ACROSS

3. St. _____: capital of Antigua & Barbados
11. Capital of Honduras
17. Capital of Bahamas
18. Port-of-_____: capital of Trinidad & Tobago
19. Capital of St. Christopher (St. Kitts) & Nevis
20. San _____: capital of Costa Rica
21. Santo _____: capital of Dominican Republic
22. Capital of St. Vincent & the Grenadines

DOWN

1. Saint _____: capital of Grenada
2. Capital of Barbados
4. San _____: capital of El Salvador
5. Capital of Dominica
6. Capital of Mexico: _____ City
7. Capital of Nicaragua
8. Capital of Canada
9. Capital of Belize
10. _____ City: capital of Guatemala
12. _____ City: capital of Panama
13. Port-au-_____: capital of Haiti
14. Capital of St. Lucia
15. Capital of Cuba
16. Capital of Jamaica
21. Washington _____: capital of the United States

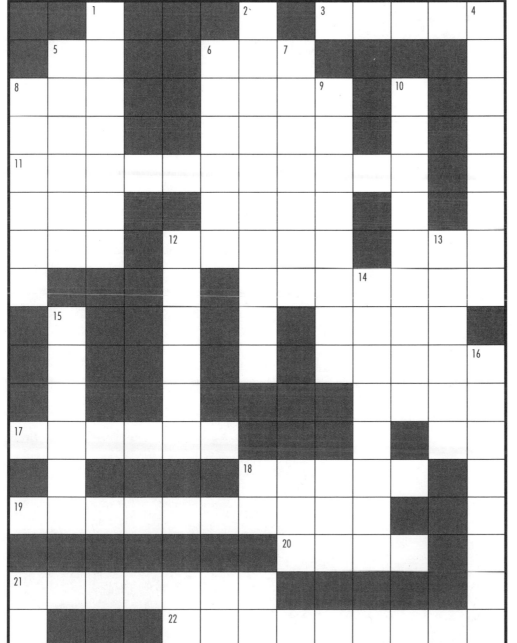

Ottawa National Arts Centre

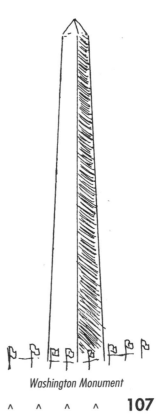

Washington Monument

^ ^

Name _____   Date _____

CROSSWORD PUZZLE

ACROSS

4. Island (affiliated with Great Britain): east of North Carolina, USA

6. _____ Rico (affiliated with the USA): east of Dominican Republic

7. _____ Antilles (affiliated with the Netherlands): east of Aruba; north of Venezuela, South America

9. _____ & Caicos Islands (affiliated with Great Britain); east of the Bahamas; north of Dominican Republic

10. Island (affiliated with Great Britain): north of St. Christopher (St. Kitts) & Nevis; northwest of Antigua & Barbuda

13. St. _____ & Miquelon Island (affiliated with France): south of Newfoundland and near the coast

14. The world's largest island (affiliated with Denmark): northeast of Canada; west of Iceland

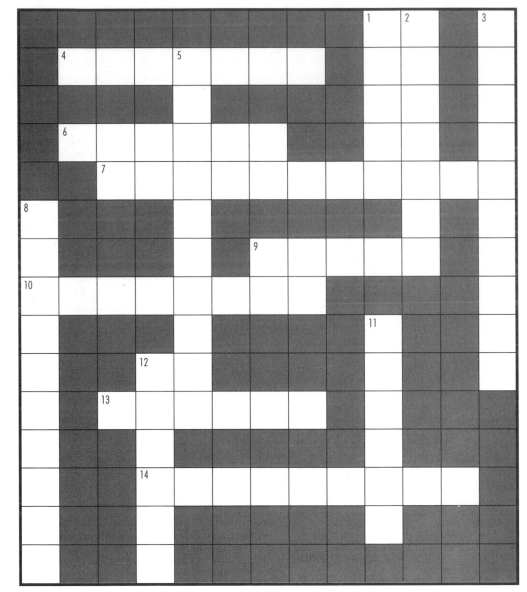

DOWN

1. An island (affiliated with the Netherlands): northwest of Venezuela in the Caribbean Sea; near the northern tip of Colombia

2. Virgin _____ (affiliated with Great Britain): east of Puerto Rico

3. An island (affiliated with Great Britain): northeast of Guadeloupe; southwest of Antigua and Barbuda

5. An island (affiliated with France): south of Dominica; north of St. Lucia

8. An island (affiliated with France): north of Dominica; southeast of Montserrat

11. Islands (affiliated with Great Britain): south of Cuba; northwest of Jamaica

12. _____ Islands (affiliated with the USA): east of Puerto Rico

Farm

^ ^

Name _____ Date _____

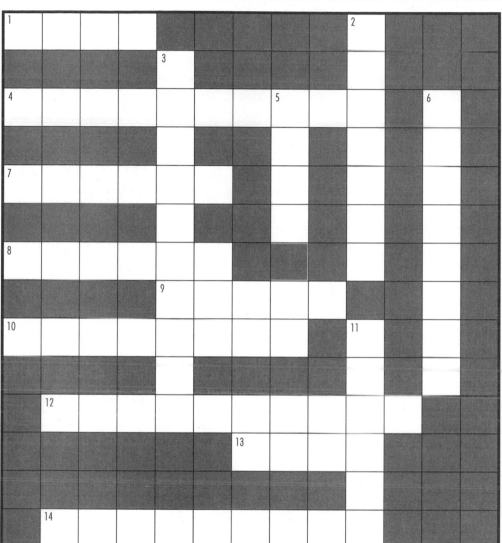

Charlotte Amalie

Godthab

CROSSWORD PUZZLE

ACROSS

1. Capital of Puerto Rico: San _____
4. Capital of Netherlands Antilles
7. Capital of St. - Pierre and Miquelon: St. - _____
8. Capital of Anguilla: The _____
9. Capital of Guadeloupe: Basse - _____
10. Capital of Montserrat
12. Capital of Aruba
13. Capital of the Virgin Islands (British): Road _____
14. Capital of the Virgin Islands (U.S.): _____ Amalie

DOWN

2. Capital of Greenland
3. Capital of Cayman Islands
5. Capital of Turks and Caicos: Grand _____
6. Capital of Bermuda
11. Capital of Martinique: Fort - de - _____

Hamilton

San Juan Fortress

^ ^

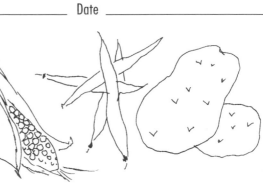

Produce

SUPPLY THE VOWEL

DIRECTIONS

This grid contains hidden words. The hidden words appear in bold print in the list below. The words can go up, down, across, at angles, backward, or forward. Parts of words may overlap. Supply the correct vowel—
a e i o u—for the center of each word group.

apples
bananas
barley
beans
berries
cherries
coffee
corn
grapes
milk
oranges
peanuts
potatoes
poultry
rice
sheep
sorghum
soybeans
sugar
wheat

C	F	B	B	T	I	B	G	J	Q	U	W	A
M	L	O	◯	P	P	L	E	S	Y	A	B	V
P	S	E	R	N	K	T	N	R	F	S	D	E
D	H	R	L	G	A	B	O	M	R	E	C	N
W	S	D	E	R	C	N	S	T	M	◯	L	K
E	G	N	Y	A	S	H	A	U	R	R	E	L
H	I	H	A	P	E	N	F	S	P	R	K	S
C	O	F	F	◯	E	J	A	G	S	E	Y	V
W	B	D	P	S	B	H	F	E	J	H	I	E
Y	L	M	A	O	T	B	G	U	B	C	S	K
C	R	N	Y	R	P	E	I	J	D	Y	E	C
O	S	T	K	G	S	E	G	N	A	R	◯	R
A	R	M	L	H	S	T	S	E	G	R	T	S
P	E	A	N	◯	T	S	I	K	N	M	A	P
O	U	W	G	M	O	C	W	S	P	U	T	R
V	Y	A	B	H	F	P	J	N	B	W	O	N
L	R	E	D	F	A	L	O	T	A	Y	P	H

Name _____ Date _____

WORD SEARCHING

DIRECTIONS

This grid contains hidden words. The hidden words appear in bold print in the list below. They can go up, down, across, at an angle, forward, or backward.

United States

Champlain

(Great) **Salt**

Michigan

Okeechobee

Tahoe

United States and Canada

Erie

Huron

Ontario

Superior

Canada

Athabasca

(Great) **Bear**

(Great) **Slave**

Manitoba

Reindeer

(Southern) **Indian**

Williston

Winnipeg

Central America

Managua

Nicaragua

B	H	E	J	N	O	T	S	I	L	L	I	W
M	A	N	I	T	O	B	A	N	D	O	N	K
I	G	E	P	I	N	N	I	W	M	I	O	A
F	L	C	Q	S	T	A	H	O	E	R	Y	G
T	U	A	C	E	L	P	K	M	D	A	F	A
L	J	S	U	P	E	R	I	O	R	T	Y	L
A	W	P	M	I	C	H	I	G	A	N	R	B
S	R	A	F	O	B	N	V	D	W	O	H	E
U	H	N	I	C	A	R	A	G	U	A	N	E
C	U	G	S	E	J	A	R	A	T	B	A	B
H	R	S	L	A	V	E	D	H	R	C	I	O
P	O	K	I	C	E	G	A	I	E	Y	D	H
I	N	T	O	D	S	B	D	S	B	J	N	C
T	M	F	N	T	A	N	H	L	E	R	I	E
G	U	I	T	S	B	R	S	Y	A	U	K	E
W	E	M	C	L	N	A	O	C	R	V	B	K
R	M	A	N	A	G	U	A	Q	D	W	P	O

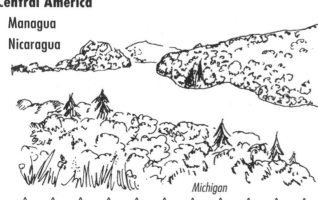

Michigan

Idaho

NORTH AMERICA RIVERS

Name _____ Date _____

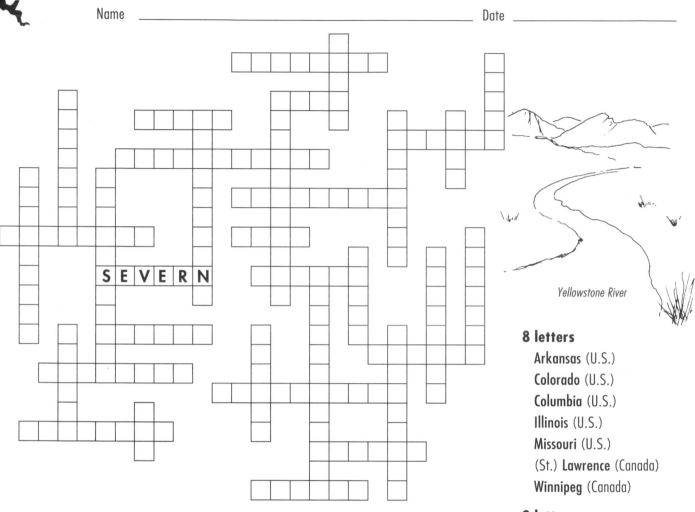

S E V E R N

Yellowstone River

CROSSING OVER

DIRECTIONS

Use a pencil for this game. Find words from the following list (the words not in parentheses) that have the correct number of spaces and letters to fit into the crossing-over boxes. Each word has a place where it belongs. The first word is done for you. To continue, find a 10-letter word with "n" in the ninth space, and so on. All the words tell about rivers on the North American continent.

3 letters
Red (Canada and U.S.)

4 letters
Back (Canada)
Coco (Central America)
Ohio (U.S.)

5 letters
Peace (Canada)
Pelly (Canada)
Snake (U. S.)
Yukon (U.S. and Canada)

6 letters
Albany (Canada)
Hudson (U.S.)
Nelson (Canada)
Ottawa (Canada)
Patuca (Central America)
Platte (U.S.)
(Rio) Grande (U.S. and Mexico)
Severn (Canada)
Wabash (U.S.)

7 letters
Motagua (Central America)

8 letters
Arkansas (U.S.)
Colorado (U.S.)
Columbia (U.S.)
Illinois (U.S.)
Missouri (U.S.)
(St.) Lawrence (Canada)
Winnipeg (Canada)

9 letters
Athabasca (Canada)
Churchill (Canada)
Mackenzie (Canada)

10 letters
Cumberland (U.S.)
Usumacinta (Mexico)

11 letters
Connecticut (U.S.)
Mississippi (U.S.)
Montmorency (Canada)

12 letters
Saskatchewan (Canada)

Hudson River

From *The Continents*, published by GoodYearBooks. Copyright © 1994 Jeanne and Arnold Cheyney.

P	A	Y	B	W	K	C	V	E	U	F	T	G
S	O	K	J	A	P	N	P	O	I	R	M	S
P	I	N	O	N	K	I	A	N	F	A	D	R
R	L	B	D	O	N	M	L	C	N	O	Y	O
U	A	S	P	E	N	D	M	G	E	B	Q	P
C	R	A	F	I	R	H	R	G	A	I	Y	W
E	T	F	P	A	C	O	T	L	I	R	Y	K
J	K	V	D	H	V	L	S	P	L	C	R	D
C	A	E	N	E	L	A	H	A	O	H	O	F
F	C	D	L	K	M	Y	R	T	N	O	K	P
A	C	F	D	J	U	C	K	P	G	E	C	A
E	U	J	O	S	H	U	A	E	A	T	I	N
L	C	D	O	J	P	Q	M	L	M	Z	H	J
G	T	A	W	E	F	O	H	P	I	F	C	T
N	L	C	D	K	X	F	P	A	H	O	E	W
O	T	C	E	K	C	O	L	M	E	H	E	G
L	H	A	R	J	W	K	D	B	T	L	B	H

WORD SEARCHING

DIRECTIONS

This grid contains hidden words. The hidden words appear in bold print in the list below. They can go up, down, across, at an angle, forward, or backward.

(American) **beech**
aspen
balsam (fir)
(barrel) **palm**
(Douglas) **fir**
hickory (tree)
Joshua (tree)
larch
longleaf (pine)
magnolia
mangrove (tree)
(paper) **birch**
piñon
ponderosa (pine)
(red) **maple**
redwood
(Sitka) **spruce**
(Western) **hemlock**
(Western red) **cedar**
(white) **oak**
(white) **pine**

Douglas Fir

Western Red Cedar   *Red Maple*   *Barrel Palm*   *Paper Birch*

Name _____ Date _____

CROSSING OVER

DIRECTIONS

Use a pencil for this game. Find words from the following list (the words not in parentheses) that have the correct number of spaces and letters to fit into the crossing-over boxes. Each word has a place where it belongs. The first word is done for you. To continue, find a 7-letter word with "o" in the sixth space, and so on. All the words name North American wild animals.

2 letters
(musk) **ox**

3 letters
(snowy) **owl**

4 letters
(fur) **seal**
(horned) **toad**
mink
(mountain) **lion**
(mule) **deer**
(Rocky Mountain) **goat**
(timber) **wolf**
(wood) **duck**

5 letters
(bighorn) **sheep**
bison
black (bear)
(Canada) **goose**
(humpback) **whale**
moose
polar (bear)
(sea) **otter**
skunk

6 letters
beaver
bobcat
coyote
iguana
(Jack) **rabbit**
Kodiak (bear)
(snapping) **turtle**
(wild) **turkey**

Roadrunner

Bald Eagle

7 letters
(American white) **pelican**
caribou
(gila) **monster**
grizzly (bear)
opossum
(prairie) **chicken**

8 letters
flamingo (bird)
(pronghorn) **antelope**

9 letters
alligator
armadillo
porcupine
wolverine

10 letters
roadrunner
sidewinder (snake)

11 letters
(diamondback) **rattlesnake**

Raccoon

Mule Deer   *Kodiak Bear*   *Bighorn Sheep*

From *The Continents*, published by GoodYearBooks. Copyright © 1994 Jeanne and Arnold Cheyney.

Name _____ Date _____

15. Nova _____: the province south of Prince Edward island
16. Newfoundland (abbr.)
18. New _____: the province west of Prince Edward Island; south of Quebec
19. The province east of Alberta; west of Manitoba
20. Saskatchewan (abbr.)
21. Nova Scotia (abbr.)
22. Prince Edward Island (abbr.)

DOWN

2. _____ Edward Island: north of Nova Scotia; east of New Brunswick
3. Yukon Territory (abbr.)
6. _____ Territories: east of Yukon Territory
7. The province east of British Columbia; west of Saskatchewan
8. Northwest Territories (abbr.)
10. _____ Territory: west of Northwest Territories; north of British Columbia
11. British _____: west of Alberta; south of Yukon Territory
13. New Brunswick (abbr.)
14. Alberta (abbr.)
17. Manitoba (abbr.)

CROSSWORD PUZZLE

Newfoundland

ACROSS

1. British Columbia (abbr.)
4. The province west of Quebec; east of Manitoba
5. Ontario (abbr.)
6. Province east of Quebec
9. The province east of Ontario; west of Newfoundland
12. The province east of Saskatchewan; west of Ontario

Saskatchewan

Name _____ Date _____

Restored Area, Halifax

St. Johns

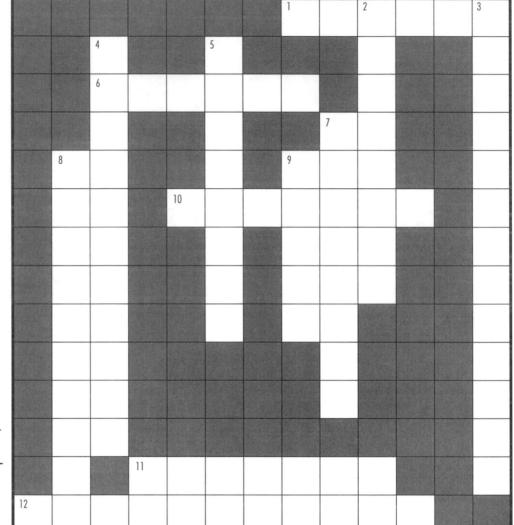

CROSSWORD PUZZLE

ACROSS

1. Capital of Quebec
6. Capital of Saskatchewan
10. Capital of Ontario
11. Capital of Nova Scotia
12. Capital of Northwest Territories

DOWN

2. Capital of Alberta
3. Capital of Prince Edward Island
4. Capital of New Brunswick
5. Capital of British Columbia
7. Capital of Manitoba
8. Capital of Yukon Territory
9. Capital of Newfoundland: St. _____

Fredericton

Winnipeg Art Gallery

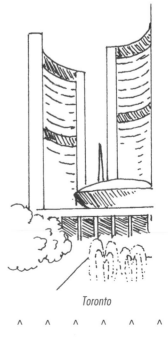

Toronto

From *The Continents*, published by GoodYearBooks. Copyright © 1994 Jeanne and Arnold Cheyney.

Name _____ Date _____

NAME SOMETHING SPECIAL ABOUT CANADA

DIRECTIONS

Fill in the dotted lines with your answers. If they are correct, the circled letters will spell something special about Canada.

1. National capital

2. British Columbia: tallest pole ever carved (80 feet)

3. Northern-border ocean

4. Each fall _____ _____ go into Churchill (town) and raid garbage cans.

5. Southwest British Columbia has _____ to keep out flood waters.

6. Eskimos and Indians now live in _____ (dwellings).

7. Manitoba: thousands of garter _____ hibernate (in lime pit)

8. French-speaking province

9. Canada: 12 _____ and 2 territories

10. Many Eskimos and Indians travel by _____ on the snow.

11. Canada: a leading _____ nation (a word for making products)

12. Newfoundland: one of the world's best fishing areas is _____

13. Prince Edward Island: 3 houses made from glass

14. A winter ice sport

15. Eastern border ocean

16. Ontario: leading _____ province (a word for growing crops)

17. First permanent Canadian settlement

18. Most-western province

19. Yukon's capital (founded during the Klondike gold rush)

20. An Arctic animal on the water

21. Eskimos and Indians now travel by _____.

22. Daily in Vancouver, at 9:00 P.M., a gun booms the _____.

23. An eastern province

24. Arctic Islands: no _____ grow

25. 1600s: _____ traders explored Ontario.

26. Northwest Territory capital

Guard

Name _____ Date _____

CROSSING OVER

DIRECTIONS

Use a pencil for this game. Find words from the following list (the words not in parentheses) that have the correct number of spaces and letters to fit into the crossing-over boxes. Each word has a place where it belongs. The first word is done for you. To continue, find an eleven-letter word with an "a" in the third space, and so on. All the words tell about Canada.

3 letters

elk

hay

(natural) **gas**

(world's largest Easter) **egg**
  (5,000 lb.)

4 letters

(1860) **gold** (discovered)

(Great) **Bear** (L.)

hogs

oats

pine (trees)

wolf

5 letters

(first Atlantic) **cable**

(Great) **Slave** (Lake)

(Manitoba) **lakes**
  (100,000)

moose

paper (forest product)

pears

Rocky (Mts.)

wheat (chief grain)

6 letters

apples

(beef) **cattle**

canoes (fur traders used)

grouse (game bird)

hockey (most popular)

Hudson (Bay)

(no trees above) timber
  (line)

Quebec (largest province)

(Royal Mounted) Police

*Alberta
World's Largest
Easter Egg*

H

S
A
L
M
O
N

salmon

(winter) **sleigh** (races)

7 letters

alfalfa (crop)

logging

Niagara (Falls)

oysters

poultry

Newfoundland

8 letters

potatoes

(St.) **Lawrence** (River)

(world's biggest) **toma-
hawk** (54-foot handle)

9 letters

petroleum

(world's first aerial)
  ambulance

*Paper Mill,
New Brunswick*

10 letters

shipwrecks (Sable Island)

11 letters

blueberries

cranberries

(1959) **snowmobiles**
  (mass produced)

(totem poles) **Thunderbird**
  (Park)

Quebec

From *The Continents*, published by GoodYearBooks. Copyright © 1994 Jeanne and Arnold Cheyney.

Name _____ Date _____

CROSSING OVER

DIRECTIONS

Use a pencil for this game. Find words from the following list (the words not in parentheses) that have the correct number of spaces and letters to fit into the crossing-over boxes. Each word has a place where it belongs. The first word is done for you. To continue, find a 5-letter word with "n" in the third space, and so on. All the words tell about Central America.

3 letters
bus (important transportation)

oak (trees)

4 letters
Coco (River)

corn

eggs

Maya (ancient Indians)

pine (trees)

rice

(San) Juan (River)

5 letters
beans

cacao (for chocolate, cocoa)

(Central America) seven (countries)

(many people) black (ancestry)

(Panama) Canal (U.S. built)

Spain (once ruled)

sugar (cane)

6 letters
coffee (a chief crop)

cotton

guavas (tropical fruit)

(many people) Indian (ancestry)

Mexico (north boundary)

shrimp (a chief catch)

soccer (a chief sport)

Drying Coffee Beans

7 letters
bananas (a chief crop)

coconut

English (language of Belize)

farmers (chief occupation)

lobster (important catch)

(many people) mulatto (black, white ancestry)

Motagua (River)

Pacific (Ocean, western border)

(rain) forests

Spanish (language of 6 countries)

8 letters
Colombia (south-border country)

mahogany (trees)

mestizos (mixed ancestry)

tropical (climate)

9 letters
Caribbean (east-border sea)

Nicaragua (largest country)

volcanoes (many active)

10 letters
pineapples

11 letters
earthquakes (some)

plantations (large estates)

Village

Banana Harvest

Name _____ Date _____

NAME SOMETHING SPECIAL ABOUT GREENLAND

DIRECTIONS

Fill in the dotted lines with your answers. If they are correct, the circled letters will spell something special about Greenland.

1. Explorers from the far northern European country of _____ probably saw Greenland first.
2. The climate is very _____.

3. Greenland is a province of _____ (a country).

4. Animals that are caught for meat and fur are _____.
5. The northern coast is near the country of _____.
6. Many people are descendants of _____ (people of a far northern frozen area).

7. The bear that is caught for meat and fur is the _____ bear.
8. Supply trucks carry _____ to people in town (a necessity).
9. The U.S. has a _____ base in Greenland.

10. The capital is _____.

11. Villagers get water from a pump, _____, or stream.
12. Important summer vegetables that are harvested are _____.
13. When the sun shines 24 hours a day in summer, it's called "The _____ Sun."

14. Long inlets of sea water between mountains are called _____.
15. Important grazing animals are _____.

16. Great chunks of ice that break off from the ice cap are called _____.
17. A southern summer crop grown for animals is _____.
18. The most important industry is _____.

19. The chief fish that is caught is the _____ fish.

1. _ _ _ ◯ _ _
2. _ ◯ _ _ _
3. _ _ _ _ _ ◯ _ _
4. _ _ _ ◯ _ _
5. _ _ _ _ ◯ _ _
6. _ ◯ _ _ _ _ _
7. _ _ ◯ _ _ _
8. _ ◯ _ _ _
9. _ _ _ _ _ _ ◯ _
10. ◯ _ _ _ _ _ _ _
11. _ _ _ ◯ _
12. _ _ _ _ _ _ _ ◯ _
13. _ _ _ _ _ _ ◯
14. _ ◯ _ _ _ _ _
15. _ ◯ _ _ _ _
16. _ ◯ _ _ _ _ _ _
17. _ ◯ _ _
18. _ _ _ _ _ ◯ _
19. _ _ ◯

Barge

Village

Dog Team

From *The Continents*, published by GoodYearBooks. Copyright © 1994 Jeanne and Arnold Cheyney.

Name _____ Date _____

MEXICO FOOD PAIRS

DIRECTIONS

All of the food pair names in the rectangle are written twice, except for one. Write the name of each food pair on a blank. (Cross off the pairs as you find them.) Then find the name of the food pair that appears only once and write it in the box.

_____   _____
_____   _____
_____   _____
_____   _____
_____   _____
_____   _____
_____   _____
_____   _____
_____   _____

MEXICO SKYSCRAPER

DIRECTIONS

Write your answers in the boxes. The circled letters will help you.

1. River on border between U.S. and Mexico: _____ Grande
2. _____ once ruled Mexico (a country).
3. A U.S. state once part of Mexico
4. Historic Indian empire
5. A public square is called a _____.
6. Spanish-style houses have _____ (courtyards).
7. A world leader in _____ mining (precious metal)
8. A leading producer of _____ (a drink)
9. A holiday meat
10. A festival is called a _____.
11. Popular game (something stuffed with presents and hit with a stick)
12. A word for hat
13. Popular musical groups with singers, trumpets, violins, guitars
14. Most popular sport

Church

From *The Continents*, published by GoodYearBooks. Copyright © 1994 Jeanne and Arnold Cheyney.

121

^ ^

Name _____ Date _____

NUMBER CODE

DIRECTIONS

Look at the number under each line. Find the matching number in the code box. Write the letter that matches that number on the corresponding answer lines.

A - 1	G - 7	M - 13	S - 19	Y - 25
B - 2	H - 8	N - 14	T - 20	Z - 26
C - 3	I - 9	O - 15	U - 21	
D - 4	J - 10	P - 16	V - 22	
E - 5	K - 11	Q - 17	W - 23	
F - 6	L - 12	R - 18	X - 24	

Market

1. Boats bring in some ___ ___ ___ ___ ___ to the islands.
   6 15 15 4 19

2. Small ___ ___ ___ ___ ___ ___   ___ ___ ___ between islands.
   16 12 1 14 5 19   6 12 25

3. Daily ___ ___ ___ ___ ___ ___ ___   ___ ___ ___ ___ between islands.
   6 5 18 18 9 5 19   19 1 9 12

4. Many houses are ___ ___ ___ ___ ___ ___ ___   ___ ___ ___ ___ ___ ___
   16 1 9 14 20 5 4   16 1 19 20 5 12

   and have ___ ___ ___ ___ ___ ___   ___ ___ ___ ___ ___   ___ ___ ___ ___ ___ ___ ___
   3 15 12 15 18 19   19 20 15 18 13   19 8 21 20 20 5 18 19

   ___ ___   ___ ___ ___ ___ ___ ___ ___ .
   15 14   23 9 14 4 15 23 19

5. Most islands were once ___ ___ ___ ___ ___ ___ ___ ___ ___ ___ .
   22 15 12 3 1 14 15 5 19

Clothing

6. Climate: ___ ___ ___ ___ ___ ___ ___ ___
   20 18 15 16 9 3 1 12

7. ___ ___ ___ ___ ___ ___ ___ ___ ___ ___   ___ ___ ___ ___ ___ ___ ___ ___ ___ ___   ___ ___ ___ .
   8 21 18 18 9 3 1 14 5 19   19 15 13 5 20 9 13 5 19   8 9 20

8. Surrounding waters of the Caribbean Sea are ___ ___ ___ ___   ___ ___ ___ ___   ___ ___ ___
   22 5 18 25   2 12 21 5   1 14 4

   ___ ___ ___ ___ ___ ___ ___ ___ ___ .
   2 5 1 21 20 9 6 21 12

9. Most people are ___ ___ ___ ___   ___ ___ ___ ___ ___ ___ ___ and live in ___ ___ ___ ___ .
   16 15 15 18   6 1 18 13 5 18 19   8 21 20 19

10. Foods: ___ ___ ___ ___ ___ , ___ ___ ___ ___ ___ , ___ ___ ___ ___ , ___ ___ ___ ___ ,
    2 5 1 14 19   3 18 1 2 19   6 9 19 8   18 9 3 5

    ___ ___ ___ ___ ___   ___ ___ ___ ___ ___ ___ ___ ___ , ___ ___ ___ ___ ___ ___ ,
    19 23 5 5 20   16 15 20 1 20 15 5 19   2 1 14 1 14 1 19

    ___ ___ ___ ___ ___ ___ ___ , ___ ___ ___ ___ ___ ___ ___
    13 1 14 7 15 5 19   15 18 1 14 7 5 19

11. Recreation: ___ ___ ___ ___ ___ , ___ ___ ___ ___ ___ ___ ,
    13 21 19 9 3   19 15 3 3 5 18

    ___ ___ ___ ___ ___ ___ ___ ___ ___ ___ , ___ ___ ___ ___ ___ ___ ___ ___ ,
    3 15 3 11 6 9 7 8 20 19   2 1 19 5 2 1 12 12

    ___ ___ ___ ___ ___ ___ ___ ___ ___ ___ , ___ ___ ___ ___ ___ ___ ___
    2 1 19 11 5 20 2 1 12 12   3 18 9 3 11 5 20

Volcanic Island

^ ^

^ ^

Name _____ Date _____

EASTERN-AREA STATES
CROSSWORD PUZZLE

New York

16. A peninsula south of Alabama and Georgia
17. State north of North Carolina; east of Kentucky; south of West Virginia

DOWN

1. _____ Virginia: south of Ohio, Pennsylvania, and Maryland
3. State east of Alabama; west of South Carolina
4. State south of Pennsylvania; north of Virginia
6. _____ Carolina: state east of Tennessee; south of Virginia; north of Georgia and South Carolina
8. State north of Connecticut and Rhode Island; east of New York; south of New Hampshire
9. State in the farthest north corner of the U. S.; northeast of New Hampshire
10. State west of New Hampshire; east of New York; north of Massachusetts
12. _____ Carolina: state northeast of Georgia; south of North Carolina
15. Rhode _____: south and west of Massachusetts; east of Connecticut

ACROSS

2. New _____: state north of Pennsylvania
5. State north of Maryland and Delaware; west of New Jersey
7. New _____: state south of New York; Atlantic Ocean on east coast
11. State south of Pennsylvania; east and north of Maryland
13. New _____: state east of Vermont; west of Maine
14. State east of New York; south of Massachusetts; west of Rhode Island

^ ^

Name _____

Date _____

EASTERN-AREA CAPITALS CROSSWORD PUZZLE

ACROSS

5. Capital of Florida
6. Capital of Massachusetts
13. Capital of Rhode Island
16. Capital of Connecticut
17. Capital of South Carolina

DOWN

1. Capital of New York
2. Capital of North Carolina
3. Capital of West Virginia
4. Capital of Vermont
7. Capital of Pennsylvania
8. Capital of Maryland
9. Capital of New Jersey
10. Capital of New Hampshire
11. Capital of Virginia
12. Capital of Georgia
14. Capital of Delaware
15. Capital of Maine

Four State Birds

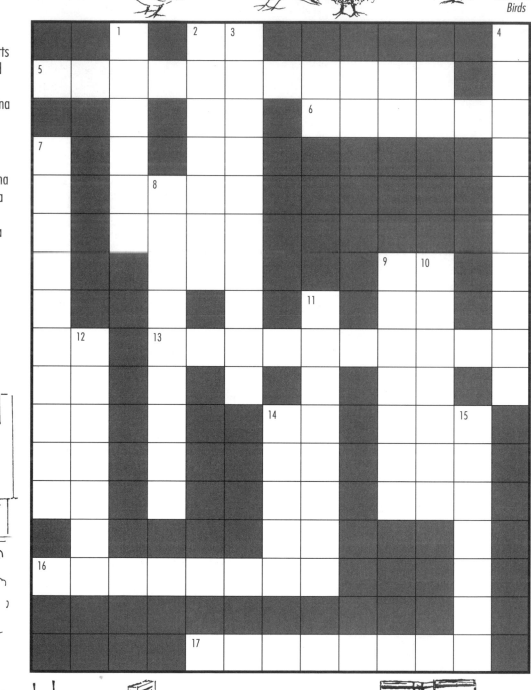

Hartford

Atlanta

Charleston

Tallahassee

From *The Continents*, published by GoodYearBooks. Copyright © 1994 Jeanne and Arnold Cheyney.

Name _____ Date _____

CENTRAL-AREA STATES CROSSWORD PUZZLE

Arkansas

DOWN

3. State west of Ohio; east of Illinois
4. State west of Wisconsin; north of Iowa
5. State south of Minnesota; east of Nebraska
6. State east of Minnesota; north of Illinois
7. State south of Kentucky; north of Mississippi, Alabama, and Georgia
8. State south of Kansas; north of Texas
9. State west of Missouri; south of Nebraska
10. State south of Iowa; north of Arkansas
11. State east of Oklahoma; west of Mississippi River
12. State bordering Lake Michigan; south of Wisconsin

ACROSS

1. State west of Georgia; east of Mississippi
2. State south of Arkansas; bordering Gulf of Mexico
4. State north of Ohio; north of Indiana
9. State south of Illinois, Indiana, Ohio; west of West Virginia
13. State bordering Lake Erie; west of Pennsylvania
14. State bordering Gulf of Mexico; south of Oklahoma
15. State bordering Gulf of Mexico; east of Mississippi River

Alamo

Name _____ Date _____

CENTRAL-AREA STATE CAPITALS CROSSWORD PUZZLE

ACROSS

1. _____ City: capital of Oklahoma
9. Capital of Illinois
12. Baton _____: capital of Louisiana
14. _____ City: capital of Missouri
16. Capital of Wisconsin
17. Capital of Michigan

DOWN

2. Capital of Texas
3. Capital of Kansas
4. Capital of Tennessee
5. Capital of Alabama
6. Des _____: capital of Iowa
7. Capital of Ohio
8. Capital of Kentucky
10. Capital of Indiana

11. Capital of Mississippi
13. St. _____: capital of Minnesota
15. Little _____: capital of Arkansas

Little Rock

From *The Continents*, published by GoodYearBooks. Copyright © 1994 Jeanne and Arnold Cheyney.

Name _____   Date _____

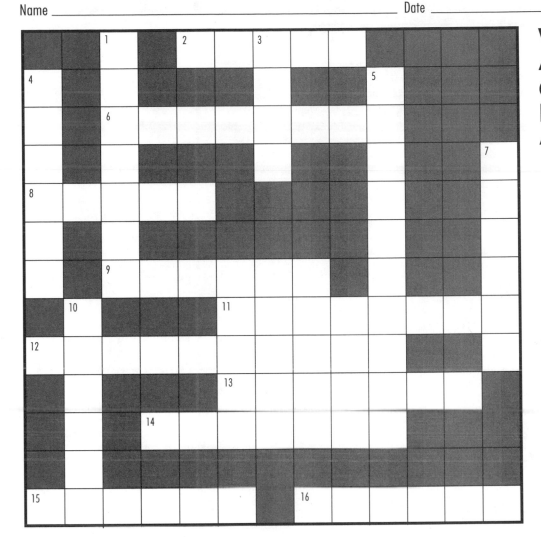

WESTERN-AREA STATES CROSSWORD PUZZLE

ACROSS

2. _____ Dakota: state south of North Dakota; north of Nebraska
6. State south of South Dakota; north of Kansas
8. State east of Washington and Oregon; west of Montana
9. State west of Canada; east of the Bering Sea
11. State east of Utah; north of New Mexico
12. State bordering Canada; north of Oregon
13. State north of Colorado; south of Montana
14. State bordering Mexico; west of New Mexico
15. State completely surrounded by water
16. State east of California; west of Utah

DOWN

1. State north of Wyoming; west of North Dakota
3. State west of Colorado; north of Arizona
4. New _____: state east of Arizona; south of Colorado
5. State west of Nevada; south of Oregon
7. State south of Washington; north of California
10. North _____: state east of Montana; north of South Dakota

Arizona

Name _____   Date _____

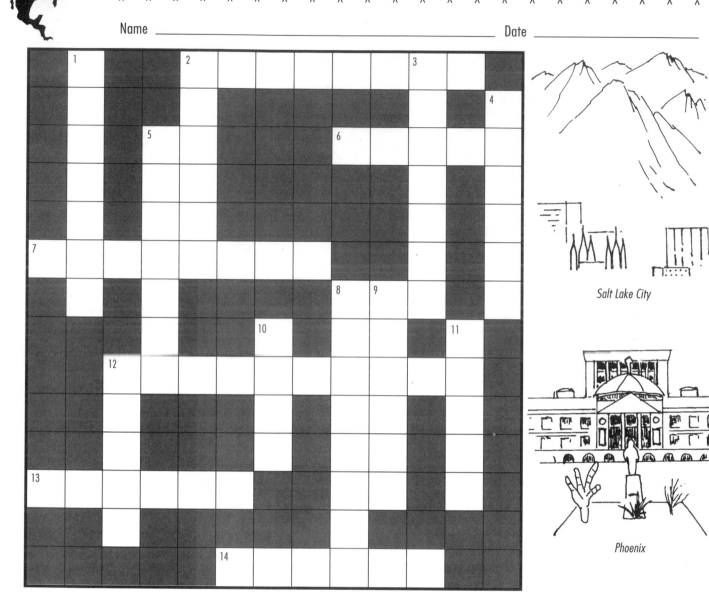

Salt Lake City

Phoenix

Boise

WESTERN- AREA STATE CAPITALS CROSSWORD PUZZLE

ACROSS

2. Capital of Hawaii
6. _____ Fe: capital of New Mexico
7. Capital of North Dakota
12. Capital of California
13. Capital of South Dakota
14. Capital of Alaska

DOWN

1. Capital of Arizona
2. Capital of Montana
3. Capital of Nebraska
4. _____ City: capital of Nevada
5. Capital of Washington
8. Capital of Wyoming
9. Capital of Colorado
10. _____ Lake City: capital of Utah
11. Capital of Idaho
12. Capital of Oregon

Santa Fe

Honolulu

Name _____ Date _____

NAME THE AMERICAN INVENTION

DIRECTIONS

Fill in the dotted lines with your answers. If they are correct, the circled letters will spell the name of an invention made by a United States citizen.

1. One-third of the U.S. is _____ land.
2. U.S. is the world's fourth-_____ country.
3. U.S. has some of the world's most _____ soil.
4. Western border ocean
5. Alexander Graham Bell invented the _____ .
6. High western mountains
7. Only one of the 5 Great Lakes totally in the U.S.
8. Eastern border ocean

9. The U.S. Naval Academy is in _____, Maryland.
10. Famous amusement park in California
11. World-famous _____ Falls (in New York)
12. Famous blind and deaf woman

13. Lowest place on U.S. land

14. _____ once roamed the western plains.
15. One of the 5 Great Lakes

16. South Florida national park

17. Kentucky: Daniel Boone founded _____ (a town)

Match Book

Earmuffs

Ice Cream

Electric Trolley

Sewing Machine

Name _____   Date _____

CROSSING OVER

DIRECTIONS

Use a pencil for this game. Find words from the following list (the words not in parentheses) that have the correct number of spaces and letters to fit into the crossing-over boxes. Each word has a place where it belongs. The first word is done for you. To continue, find a five-letter word with a "t" in the first space, and so on. All the words tell about the United States.

3 letters

hay (crop)

Kit (Carson, frontiersman)

(MI) **Soo** (Canals)

(sled) **dog** (Derby)

sun (flower seeds)

4 letters

beef (cattle)

coal

corn

(Great) **Salt** (Lake)

hogs

(ice cream) **soda** (invented)

(Liberty) **Bell**

(New) **York** (largest city)

rice

(Wyatt) **Earp** (lawman)

5 letters

(Daniel) **Boone** (frontiersman)

fifty (states)

maple (sugar)

(Mark) **Twain** (writer)

(people) **Amish** (horse-drawn carriages)

(rubber) tires

seals (world's largest herd)

wheat

6 letters

Apache (Indians)

apples

Boeing (airplane factory)

cheese

citrus (fruit)

cotton

Hoover (Dam)

(many) **Indian** (tribes)

rodeos

salmon (fish)

7 letters

(active) **diamond** (mine:

near Murfreesboro, Arkansas)

(many) **forests**

redwood (world's tallest trees)

(world's fourth) **largest** (country)

8 letters

Cherokee (Indians)

(Davy) **Crockett** (frontiersman)

football (popular)

Nautilus (world's first nuclear sub)

potatoes

9 letters

(active) **volcanoes**

Arlington (National Cemetery)

(first permanent English settlement) **Jamestown** (VA)

(St.) **Augustine** (oldest city)

10 letters

Gettysburg (Battle of)

Washington

11 letters

Appalachian (Mts.)

cranberries

Yellowstone (National Park)

12 letters

(historic village) **Williamsburg**

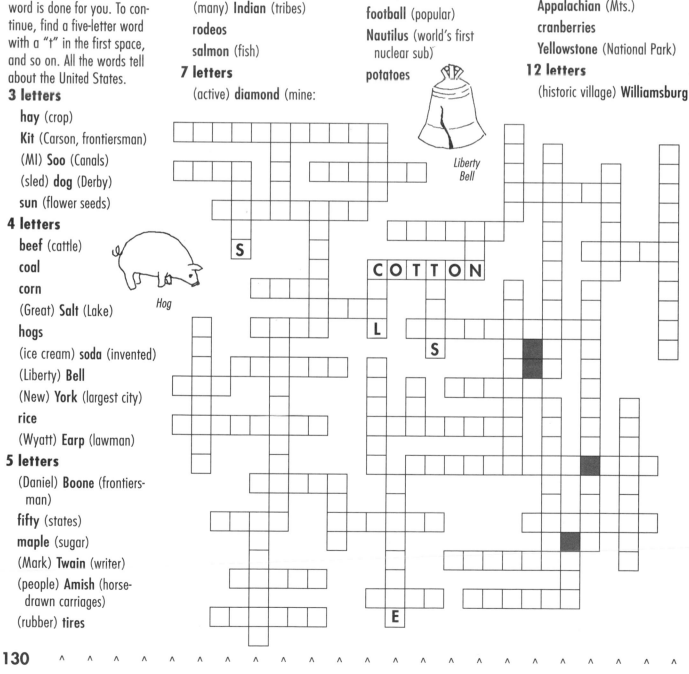

Liberty Bell

Hog

From *The Continents*, published by GoodYearBooks. Copyright © 1994 Jeanne and Arnold Cheyney.

^ ^

Name _____ Date _____

Letters visible in grid: **C**, **B A R L E Y**, **H**

Ferryliners

CROSSING OVER

DIRECTIONS

Use a pencil for this game. Find words from the following list (the words not in parentheses) that have the correct number of spaces and letters to fit into the crossing-over boxes. Each word has a place where it belongs. The first word is done for you. To continue, find a 9-letter word with "a" in the second space, and so on. All the words tell about Alaska.

3 letters

dog (sled races)

elk

hay

oil (chief wealth)

(summer) sun (20 hours a day)

(trappers) fur (industry)

4 letters

deer

hogs

milk (a chief product)

moss (far north)

oats

5 letters

birch (tree)

(brown) bears

crops (grown up to Arctic Circle)

fruit

moose

polar (bears)

seals (world's most seals)

sheep

Yukon (chief river)

6 letters

(bald) eagles (world's largest number)

barley

Barrow (most N. city)

cattle

(1867) Seward (bought Alaska)

(51 miles to) Russia

Juneau (capital)

Kodiak (Island bears)

lichen

(1/3 above) Arctic (Circle)

planes (to all parts of Alasku)

salmon

shrimp

(Sitka) spruce (state tree)

(southwest) Bering (Sea)

Seal

7 letters

(Alaska) Highway

caribou

Chilkat (R., eagles gather by it)

Eskimos

Indians

largest (U.S. state)

(many) forests

Prudhoe (Bay; oil)

(wild) flowers

8 letters

glaciers

(islands) Pribilof (most seals)

(Mt.) McKinley (highest in North America)

potatoes

reindeer (meat, hides)

(southwest) Aleutian (Islands)

9 letters

(city) Anchorage (most people)

(valley) Matanuska (most crops)

volcanoes (many active)

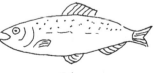

Salmon

Name _____ Date _____

NUMBER CODE

DIRECTIONS

Look at the number under each line. Find the matching number in the code box. Write the letter that matches that number on the corresponding answer lines.

A - 1	G - 7	M - 13	S - 19	Y - 25
B - 2	H - 8	N - 14	T - 20	Z - 26
C - 3	I - 9	O - 15	U - 21	
D - 4	J - 10	P - 16	V - 22	
E - 5	K - 11	Q - 17	W - 23	
F - 6	L - 12	R - 18	X - 24	

1. Location: ___ ___ ___ ___ ___ ___ ___ ___ ___ of the U.S.
19 15 21 20 8 23 5 19 20

2. Climate: ___ ___ ___ ___ ___ ___ ___ ___ ___ ___ ___
13 9 12 4 1 12 12 25 5 1 18

3. Capital and largest city: ___ ___ ___ ___ ___ ___ ___ ___
8 15 14 15 12 21 12 21

4. Original settlers: ___ ___ ___ ___ ___ ___ ___ ___ ___ ___ ___
16 15 12 25 14 5 19 9 1 14 19

5. Hawaii: ___ ___ ___ ___ ___ ___ ___ ___ ___ ___ . ___ ___ ___ ___ ___
25 15 21 14 7 5 19 20 21 19 19 20 1 20 5

6. The U.S. ___ ___ ___ ___ ___ ___ ___ ___ ___ ___ ___ ___ ___ ___ ___
16 1 3 9 6 9 3 13 9 12 9 20 1 18 25
___ ___ ___ ___ ___ ___ ___ ___ ___ ___ ___
3 15 13 13 1 14 4 2 1 19 5 is in Hawaii.

7. The Hawaiian alphabet has ___ ___ ___ ___ ___ ___ ___ ___ ___ ___ ___ ___ ___
20 23 5 12 22 5 12 5 20 20 5 18 19
(___ ___ ___ ___ ___ ___ ___ ___ ___ ___ ___ ___).
1 5 8 9 11 12 13 14 15 16 21 23

8. Hawaii has ___ ___ ___ ___ ___ ___ ___ ___ ___ ___ ___ ___ ___ ___ ___ .
1 3 20 9 22 5 22 15 12 3 1 14 15 5 19

9. World's largest inactive volcano: ___ ___ ___ ___ ___ ___ ___ ___ ___ ___ ___ ___ ___ ___ ___
8 1 12 5 1 11 1 12 1 3 18 1 20 5 18
(about 20 miles around, 3,000 ft. deep)

10. Favorite activity: ___ ___ ___ ___ ___ ___ ___ ___ ___ ___ ___
23 1 20 5 18 19 16 15 18 20 19

11. Words: ___ ___ ___ ___ (feast), ___ ___ ___ ___ (dance),
12 21 1 21 8 21 12 1
___ ___ ___ ___ ___ ___ ___ (leaping flea), ___ ___ ___ (wreath)
21 11 21 12 5 12 5 12 5 9

12. Lanai Island: ___ ___ ___ ___ ___ ___ ___ ___ ___ ___ ___ ___ ___ ___ on about 98%
16 9 14 5 1 16 16 12 5 19 7 18 15 23
of the cultivated land (for Dole products)

13. Some crops: ___ ___ ___ ___ , ___ ___ ___ ___ ___ ___ , ___ ___ ___ ___ ___ ___ ___
20 1 18 15 7 21 1 22 1 19 2 1 14 1 14 1 19

Diamond Head Beach

Hibiscus Flower

Polynesian Dancer

Totem Pole

From The Continents, published by GoodYearBooks. Copyright © 1994 Jeanne and Arnold Cheyney.

Name _____ Date _____

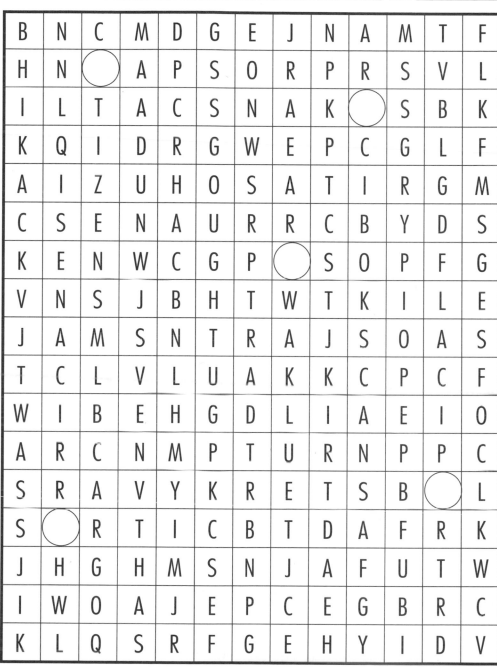

B	N	C	M	D	G	E	J	N	A	M	T	F
H	N	◯	A	P	S	O	R	P	R	S	V	L
I	L	T	A	C	S	N	A	K	◯	S	B	K
K	Q	I	D	R	G	W	E	P	C	G	L	F
A	I	Z	U	H	O	S	A	T	I	R	G	M
C	S	E	N	A	U	R	R	C	B	Y	D	S
K	E	N	W	C	G	P	◯	S	O	P	F	G
V	N	S	J	B	H	T	W	T	K	I	L	E
J	A	M	S	N	T	R	A	J	S	O	A	S
T	C	L	V	L	U	A	K	K	C	P	C	F
W	I	B	E	H	G	D	L	I	A	E	I	O
A	R	C	N	M	P	T	U	R	N	P	P	C
S	R	A	V	Y	K	R	E	T	S	B	◯	L
S	◯	R	T	I	C	B	T	D	A	F	R	K
J	H	G	H	M	S	N	J	A	F	U	T	W
I	W	O	A	J	E	P	C	E	G	B	R	C
K	L	Q	S	R	F	G	E	H	Y	I	D	V

Church of San José

SUPPLY THE VOWEL

DIRECTIONS

This grid contains hidden words. The hidden words appear in bold print in the list to the right. The words can go up, down, across, at angles, backward, or forward. Parts of words may overlap. Supply the correct vowel—a e i o u—for the center of each word group.

Arecibo (a long river)

(breed of horses) **Paso** (Fino)

cattle

citrus (fruits)

coffee

eggs

(first-known settlers) **Arawak** (Indians)

hurricanes

kapok (tree)

lobster (chief catch)

milk (very important)

(Puerto Ricans) **citizens** (of U.S.)

rain (forests)

(San) **Juan** (capital)

(sea) **grapes** (fruit)

snakes

Spain (once ruled)

star (apple)

sugar (cane)

tropical (climate)

SOUTH AMERICA

Caribbean Sea

ATLANTIC OCEAN

Caracas

L. Maracaibo

Orinoco R.

10° N

VENEZUELA

Georgetown
Paramaribo
Cayenne

Bogotá

SURINAME

COLOMBIA

GUYANA

French Guiana

Magdalena R.

ECUADOR

Quito

Equator 0°

Galápagos Is. (Ec.)

Amazon R.

BRAZIL

PERU

ANDES

10° S

Lima

Brasília

São Francisco R.

L. Titicaca

La Paz

BOLIVIA

BRAZILIAN

Sucre

HIGHLANDS

L. Poópo

Paraguay R.

PACIFIC OCEAN

ATACAMA DESERT

PARAGUAY

Paraná R.

20° S

Río de Janeiro

Asunción

São Paulo

ANDES

Paraná R.

Uruguay R.

CHILE

Santiago

URUGUAY

L. Mirim

30° S

Buenos Aires

Montevideo

ATLANTIC OCEAN

ARGENTINA

PATAGONIA

40° S

Falkland Is. (U.K.)

Stanley

SCALE

0	500	1000 Miles

0	500	1000 Kilometers

Azimuthal Equal–Area Projection

Cape Horn

100° W   90° W   80° W   70° W   60° W   50° W   40° W   30° W   20° W

From *The Continents*, published by GoodYearBooks. Copyright © 1994 Jeanne and Arnold Cheyney.

Name _____ Date _____

25. Southern-most tip of South America: Cape _____

DOWN

1. South of the equator: December to June is _____ (season).
2. Central _____: covers 3/5 of South America
3. The high Andes' peaks are very _____ (temperature).
4. Initials for South America
5. _____ American Highway links all the national highways in South America.
6. Andes valleys and plateaus: abundant grass for sheep and _____
7. South America: _____-largest continent
9. Tropical Rain Forest covers one-_____ of South America
12. South of the equator: June to December is _____ (season)
13. Ocean bordering western South America
15. Important means of transportation (inland, rugged, and remote areas)
16. Sea bordering northern South America
20. Animals that can carry heavy loads

CROSSWORD PUZZLE

ACROSS

8. One of the world's driest places: _____ Desert
10. World's largest tropical _____ forest
11. Tropical Rain Forest: _____ and wet all year
14. Eastern boundary of South America: _____ Ocean
17. Telephones are found mostly in _____, not remote areas.
18. South America: almost totally surrounded by _____
19. Precious metal found in Andes Mountains: _____
21. Imaginary line running around the middle of the earth: _____
22. A coastal fish
23. Very fine, long, silky wool comes from these animals.
24. Rugged mountain range that runs along the western border: _____

Andes Mountains

INDEPENDENT COUNTRIES AND POLITICAL UNITS

Name _____ Date _____

CROSSWORD PUZZLE

ACROSS

2. Long, narrow country west of Argentina
3. Country connecting South America with Central America
5. Country bordered by Argentina, Bolivia, and Brazil
7. Country east of Surinam; north of Brazil: French _____
8. Country west of Brazil; east of Peru
12. Country bordering North Atlantic Ocean; between Guyana and French Guiana
13. Country bordering Pacific Ocean; north of Chile; south of Ecuador and Columbia
14. Country east of Venezuela and west of Suriname

DOWN

1. Country south of Colombia; north of Peru
4. The largest country in South America
6. British dependency islands near the southern Argentina coast; _____ Islands
9. Country bordering South Atlantic Ocean; east of Chile
10. Country bordering Caribbean Sea; east of Colombia
11. Country bordering Atlantic Ocean; east of Argentina; south of Brazil

Village Hut

From *The Continents*, published by GoodYearBooks. Copyright © 1994 Jeanne and Arnold Cheyney.

CAPITALS OF INDEPENDENT COUNTRIES AND POLITICAL UNITS

SOUTH AMERICA

From *The Continents*, published by GoodYearBooks. Copyright © 1994 Jeanne and Arnold Cheyney.

Name _____ Date _____

Brasilia

Caracas

CROSSWORD PUZZLE

ACROSS

3. Actual capital of Bolivia: La _____ (seat of government)
5. Capital of Argentina; _____ Aires
6. Capital of Guyana
8. Capital of Venezuela
9. Official capital of Bolivia
10. Capital of Falkland Islands (British); Port _____
11. Capital of Uruguay
13. Capital of Brazil
14. Capital of (French) Guiana

DOWN

1. Capital of Colombia
2. Capital of Ecuador
4. Capital of Paraguay
7. Capital of Suriname
9. Capital of Chile
12. Capital of Peru

Santiago

SOUTH AMERICA FISHING CATCHES, RIVERS, OCEANS, SEAS, AND WATERFALLS

^ ^

Name _____ Date _____

A	S	S	B	A	N	E	L	A	D	G	A	M
D	M	E	G	A	F	G	I	K	H	E	C	A
O	A	N	L	M	N	N	J	A	C	U	A	C
Q	L	I	P	I	R	G	U	W	S	N	T	K
A	C	D	R	Y	V	H	E	O	H	A	K	E
N	A	R	C	C	G	B	O	L	E	N	F	R
C	E	A	J	A	Q	D	S	Y	I	E	N	E
H	K	S	H	R	I	M	P	K	C	U	W	L
O	P	O	T	I	L	B	M	I	O	C	A	E
V	Z	U	C	B	E	P	F	S	V	U	P	S
E	F	T	I	B	D	I	C	M	Y	C	A	R
T	G	H	Q	E	C	G	N	H	R	L	R	E
T	P	A	R	A	G	U	A	Y	U	A	A	K
A	J	W	P	N	B	A	M	A	Z	O	N	A
D	O	R	I	N	O	C	O	G	U	E	A	O
T	A	F	R	U	R	U	G	U	A	Y	H	R
J	S	V	I	K	A	T	L	A	N	T	I	C

Fishing catches:
anchovetta
clams
croakers
hake
herring
(Jack) mackerel
sardines
shrimp

Shrimp

Sea:
Caribbean

Oceans:
(North) **Atlantic**
South (Atlantic)
(South) **Pacific**

Rivers:
Amazon
Cauca
Magdalena
Orinoco
Paraguay
Paraná
São (Francisco)
Uruguay

Waterfalls

Waterfalls:
Angel
Cucuenán
Iguaçu

WORD SEARCHING

River Travel

DIRECTIONS

This grid contains hidden words. The hidden words appear in bold print in the list at the right. They can go up, down, across, at an angle, forward, or backward.

Fishing

From *The Continents*, published by GoodYearBooks. Copyright © 1994 Jeanne and Arnold Cheyney.

^ ^ ^ ^ ^ ^ ^ ^ ^ ^ ^ ^ ^ ^ ^ ^ ^

TREES, PLANTS, FLOWERS SOUTH AMERICA

Name _____   Date _____

WORD SEARCHING

DIRECTIONS

This grid contains hidden words. The hidden words appear in bold print in the list below. They can go up, down, across, at an angle, forward, or backward.

Trees:

Kapok

avocado

balsa

Brazil (nut)

cacao

cannonball

cashew

(cigar-box) **cedar**

coconut (palm)

jacaranda

kapok

logwood

mahogany

rosewood

rubber

Paper-Spine Cactus

Plants:

arrowroot

bamboo

(giant) **bromelia**

maté

Panama (hat, palm plant)

(paper-spine) **cactus**

philodendron

pineapple

Flowers:

(cattleya) **orchid** (one of many varieties)

portulaca

A	R	O	S	E	W	O	O	D	B	C	D	L
J	U	M	A	R	R	O	W	R	O	O	T	I
G	B	R	O	M	E	L	I	A	H	I	K	Z
F	B	Q	C	E	A	O	D	A	C	O	V	A
P	E	D	A	S	B	S	U	T	C	A	C	R
N	R	I	N	M	O	N	L	O	W	U	L	B
O	T	H	N	L	A	H	C	A	S	H	E	W
R	D	C	O	O	V	O	G	C	B	A	U	J
D	F	R	N	G	P	B	S	A	E	Y	D	A
N	N	O	B	W	F	A	R	C	G	N	L	C
E	V	E	A	O	B	M	A	T	E	A	I	A
D	J	M	L	O	R	B	D	Q	W	G	H	R
O	Y	C	L	D	J	O	E	L	T	O	C	A
L	T	U	N	O	C	O	C	P	Z	H	O	N
I	K	M	K	I	L	A	M	A	N	A	P	D
H	A	C	A	L	U	T	R	O	P	M	A	A
P	I	N	E	A	P	P	L	E	B	N	K	O

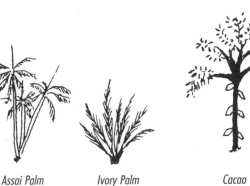

Maté

Pineapple   *Paraná Pine*   *Assai Palm*   *Ivory Palm*   *Cacao*   *Coconut Palm*

139

SOUTH AMERICA ANIMALS

Name _____ Date _____

CROSSING OVER

DIRECTIONS

Use a pencil for this game. Find words from the following list (the words not in parentheses) that have the correct number of spaces and letters to fit into the crossing-over boxes. Each word has a place where it belongs. The first word is done for you. To continue, find an 8-letter word with "b" in the fifth space, and so on. All the words tell about animals in South America.

3 letters

boa (constrictor, reptile)
(Guinea) **pig**
(Vampire) **bat**

4 letters

cavy (rodent)
(giant) **toad**
ibis (wading bird)
(maned) **wolf**
rhea (ostrich-like)
(spectacled) **bear**
(swamp) **deer**

5 letters

coati (coon-like)
egret (cattle bird)
llama (camel family)
sloth
tapir
yapok (otter-like)

6 letters

alpaca (long, silky wool)
(black) **caiman** (reptile)
iguana
jaguar
lizard
(sapajou) **monkey**
nutria (rodent)
turtle
vicuña (camel family)

7 letters

guanaco (camel family)
manatee (large water animal)
peccary (pig-like)
penguin (flightless bird)
piranha (flesh-eating fish)

8 letters

anaconda (one of the world's largest reptiles)
anteater
capybara (rodent)
flamingo (bird, pinkish red)
marmoset (small monkey)

9 letters

armadillo (bony shell)
porcupine

10 letters

bushmaster (reptile)
chinchilla (pearl-gray fur)

Flamingo

Coati

Alpaca

Piranha

Vampire Bat

Parrot

From *The Continents*, published by GoodYearBooks. Copyright © 1994 Jeanne and Arnold Cheyney.

MOUNTAINS, DAM, LAKES, AND DESERTS

SOUTH AMERICA

Name _____ Date _____

E	A	K	O	E	M	N	R	U	J	B	T	A
H	S	Q	U	P	I	A	T	I	C	I	A	R
S	A	P	I	T	S	I	M	F	V	L	P	I
Y	C	G	I	A	W	L	A	D	G	T	U	E
D	O	E	B	N	M	I	R	I	M	C	N	D
M	N	P	H	D	H	Z	F	O	W	L	G	N
A	C	K	M	E	I	A	B	P	N	Y	A	A
R	A	N	I	S	G	R	C	O	J	C	T	B
A	G	A	O	Q	H	B	G	O	P	A	O	H
C	U	R	A	N	L	I	F	P	C	A	Q	D
A	A	A	M	E	A	L	R	A	G	C	K	P
I	J	C	D	T	N	C	M	E	W	A	S	N
B	H	S	V	Y	D	A	U	Q	O	C	T	B
O	D	A	L	A	S	J	A	N	A	I	U	G
N	O	U	F	K	G	M	P	W	R	T	A	L
Y	T	H	O	Z	A	R	O	B	M	I	H	C
U	I	S	F	A	I	N	O	G	A	T	A	P

WORD SEARCHING

DIRECTIONS

This grid contains hidden words. The hidden words appear in bold print in the list below. They can go up, down, across, at an angle, forward, or backward.

Mountains:
Aconcagua
Andes
Brazilian (Highlands)
Chimborazo
(Eastern) **Highlands**
(El) **Misti**
Guiana (Highlands)
Huascarán
(Ojos del) **Salado**
(Pico da) **Bandeira**
(Sierra do) **Espinhaco**
Tapungato

Deserts:
Atacama
Patagonia

Dam:
Itaipú

Lakes:
Maracaibo
Mirim
Poopó
Titicaca

Andes Mts.

*Sugarloaf Mt.
Rio de Janeiro*

Reed Boat on Lake

141

Name _____ Date _____

DIRECTIONS

Find the latitude and longitude of each item by using maps in the encyclopedia or atlas. Write the answers in the blanks to the right.

1. 10° South Latitude, 50° West Longitude: _ _ _ _ _ _ _

2. 30° South Latitude, 60° West Longitude: _ _ _ _ _ _ _ _

3. 2° South Latitude, 80° West Longitude: _ _ _ _ _ _ _

4. 20° South Latitude, 70° West Longitude: _ _ _ _ _

5. 5° North Latitude, 65° West Longitude: _ _ _ _ _ _ _ _

6. 34° South Latitude, 56° West Longitude: _ _ _ _ _ _ _ _

7. 16° South Latitude, 64° West Longitude: _ _ _ _ _ _ _

8. 6° North Latitude, 59° West Longitude: _ _ _ _ _ _

9. 10° South Latitude, 75° West Longitude: _ _ _ _ _

10. 24° South Latitude; 56° West Longitude: _ _ _ _ _ _ _ _

11. 4° North Latitude, 56° West Longitude: _ _ _ _ _ _ _ _

12. 5° North Latitude, 75° West Longitude: _ _ _ _ _ _ _

13. 3° North Latitude, 53° West Longitude: _ _ _ _ _ _ _ _ _ _ _

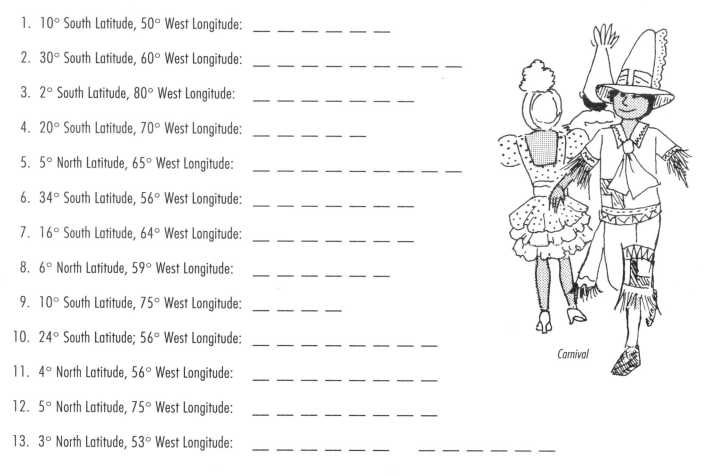

Carnival

*Reeds for a
House Roof*

Ecuador

THINGS OF INTEREST SOUTH AMERICA

Name _____ Date _____

NUMBER CODE

DIRECTIONS

Look at the number under each line. Find the matching number in the code box. Write the letter that matches that number on the answer line.

A - 1	G - 7	M - 13	S - 19	Y - 25	
B - 2	H - 8	N - 14	T - 20	Z - 26	
C - 3	I - 9	O - 15	U - 21		
D - 4	J - 10	P - 16	V - 22		
E - 5	K - 11	Q - 17	W - 23		
F - 6	L - 12	R - 18	X - 24		

1. Argentina: the Southern tip is about 600 miles from

___ ___ ___ ___ ___ ___ ___ ___ ___ ___
1 14 20 1 18 3 20 9 3 1

2. Bolivia has

___ ___ ___   ___ ___ ___ ___ ___ ___ ___ ___ .
20 23 15   3 1 16 9 20 1 12 19

Bow and Arrow Fishing

3. Brazil: Amazon Rain Forests have over 42,000 varieties of

___ ___ ___ ___ ___ ___ ,   over 3,000 kinds of
16 12 1 14 20 19

over 1,500 kinds of

___ ___ ___ ___ ___ ,   ___ ___ ___ ___ ___
20 18 5 5 19   2 9 18 4 19

4. Chile has one of the world's largest

___ ___ ___ ___ ___ ___ ___
6 9 19 8 9 14 7

___ ___ ___ ___ ___ ___ ___ ___ ___ ___ .
9 14 4 21 19 20 18 9 5 19

5. Colombia has two main attractions:

___ ___ ___ ___   ___ ___ ___ ___ ___ ,
1 21 20 15   18 1 3 5 19

___ ___ ___ ___ ___ ___ ___ ___ ___ ___
2 21 12 12 6 9 7 8 20 19

6. Ecuador has the world's highest active

___ ___ ___ ___ ___ ___ ___ ___ .
22 15 12 3 1 14 15

7. Guyana has a coastal region mostly

___ ___ ___ ___ ___   ___ ___ ___   ___ ___ ___ ___ ___ .
2 5 12 15 23   19 5 1   12 5 22 5 12

8. Paraguay: less than 2% of the people own

___ ___ ___ ___
3 1 18 19

9. Peru: the ruins of

___ ___ ___ ___ ___   ___ ___ ___ ___ ___ ___   were once a walled
13 1 3 8 21   16 9 3 3 8 21

___ ___ ___ ___   ___ ___ ___ ___ .
9 14 3 1   3 9 20 25

10. Suriname: the Rain Forest mountains have about 2,000 kinds of

___ ___ ___ ___ ___
20 18 5 5 19

11. Uruguay: a favorite cowboy meal is

___ ___ ___ ___ ___ ___ ___ ___ ___   ___ ___ ___ ___ ___ ___ ___ ,
2 1 18 2 5 3 21 5 4   19 1 21 19 1 7 5

kidneys, strips of

___ ___ ___ ___
2 5 5 6

12. Venezuela means

___ ___ ___ ___ ___ ___   ___ ___ ___ ___ ___ ___
12 9 20 20 12 5   22 5 14 9 3 5

Folk Dancer

Reed Boats

143

^ ^

Name _____ Date _____

Processing Manioc

Village Market

SUPPLY THE VOWEL

DIRECTIONS

This grid contains hidden words. The hidden words appear in bold print in the list below. The words can go up, down, across, at angles, backward, or forward. Parts of words may overlap. Supply the correct vowel—a e i o u—for the center of each word group.

bananas

(Brazil) **nuts**

cacao

citrus (fruit)

coffee

corn

cotton

grapes

manioc

maté (leaves used for tea-like drink)

oilseeds

pepper

potatoes

quebracho (tannin; for tanning hides)

rice

rubber

sheep

soybeans

sugar (cane)

wheat

Harvesting Coffee

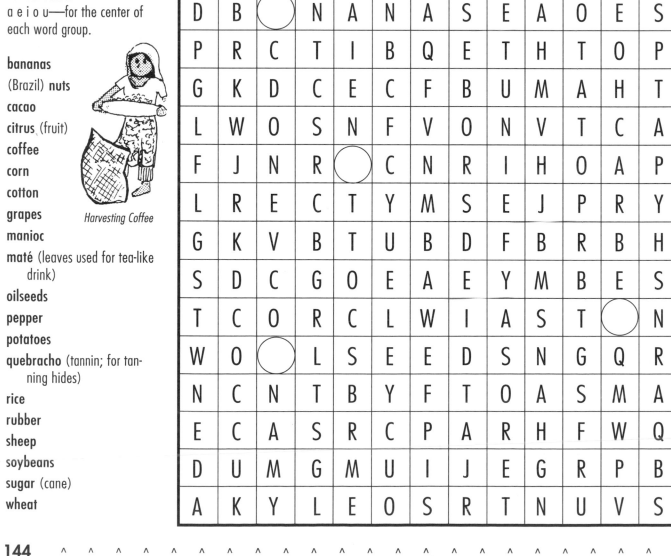

C	J	O	E	U	S	T	A	S	K	G	J	W
P	F	A	H	E	O	Q	M	K	H	S	H	I
L	M	C	P	N	F	R	E	P	P	○	P	R
D	B	○	N	A	N	A	S	E	A	O	E	S
P	R	C	T	I	B	Q	E	T	H	T	O	P
G	K	D	C	E	C	F	B	U	M	A	H	T
L	W	O	S	N	F	V	O	N	V	T	C	A
F	J	N	R	○	C	N	R	I	H	O	A	P
L	R	E	C	T	Y	M	S	E	J	P	R	Y
G	K	V	B	T	U	B	D	F	B	R	B	H
S	D	C	G	O	E	A	E	Y	M	B	E	S
T	C	O	R	C	L	W	I	A	S	T	○	N
W	O	○	L	S	E	E	D	S	N	G	Q	R
N	C	N	T	B	Y	F	T	O	A	S	M	A
E	C	A	S	R	C	P	A	R	H	F	W	Q
D	U	M	G	M	U	I	J	E	G	R	P	B
A	K	Y	L	E	O	S	R	T	N	U	V	S

^ ^

^ ^

Name _____ Date _____

CROSSWORD PUZZLE

ACROSS

1. A beverage crop
4. The fertile plain covering about 1/5 of the country
5. People of mixed Indian and European ancestry
7. A chief grain crop
8. Western border mountains
9. A pampa livestock
10. Argentine cowboy
12. Most popular sport
14. A chief export
15. A chief farm crop: sugar_____
17. Most of the north is covered with _____.
18. A chief farm crop: _____seed
19. A chief animal product export
20. A favorite sport, similar to polo
22. _____ once ruled Argentina.
23. Capital and largest city: _____ Aires
25. A chief dairy product
26. Most popular beverage
27. The first settlers searched for _____.
28. Spectacular waterfalls

Gauchos

DOWN

2. Entire eastern border: _____ Ocean
3. A chief food and grain crop
6. Dry, windy southern plateau
11. A chief export: vegetable _____
13. Colorful festival held before Lent
16. A chief livestock export
21. A chief food product crop: _____flower seeds
23. Most popular meat
24. Argentina produces nearly all its own _____ (mineral).

From *The Continents*, published by GoodYearBooks. Copyright © 1994 Jeanne and Arnold Cheyney.

^ ^

Name _____ Date _____

CROSSING OVER

DIRECTIONS

Use a pencil for this game. Find words from the following list (the words not in parentheses) that have the correct number of spaces and letters to fit into the crossing-over boxes. Each word has a place where it belongs. The first word is done for you. To continue, find a 6-letter word with a "g" in the second space, and so on. All the words tell about Brazil.

3 letters

bus (most people's transportation)

(large city) **Rio** (de Janeiro)

raw (sugar)

4 letters

(Brazil, nearly) **half** (of continent)

(Brazil) **nuts**

(important food) **rice**

(N.E.) **soil** (poor)

rain (forest)

5 letters

(black) **beans**

(lowland, jungle) **selva**

(São) **Paulo** (large city)

6 letters

Amazon (River)

coffee (world leader)

cotton

Iguaçu (Falls)

Itaipú (Dam)

lemons

Paraná (R.)

quartz (world leader)

7 letters

bananas

cassava (root)

gauchos (cowboys)

largest (South American country)

lobster

(most of Brazil) **tropics**

oranges

papayas (fruit)

ranches

8 letters

Atlantic (eastern border)

Brasilia (capital)

carnauba (tree for wax)

10 letters

(official langauge)
Portuguese

11 letters

butterflies

nordestinos (people of N.E. region)

Praying

Desert

Spinning Cotton Thread

From *The Continents*, published by GoodYearBooks. Copyright © 1994 Jeanne and Arnold Cheyney.

Name _____   Date _____

Clothing

B
A
N
A
N
A
S

Transportation

6 letters
ajiaco (favorite soup)
Bogotá (capital)
cotton
llanos (flat grassland)
(many) **cattle**
Panamá (connects to Venezuela)
ruanas (wool blanket cape)
soccer (favorite sport)

7 letters
bananas
cassava (root crop)
(colorful) **textile** (industry)
equator (through Venezuela)

8 letters
emeralds (90 percent of world's)
mestizos (mixed ancestry)
(named for) **Columbus**
potatoes
tugurios (slums)
volcanos (active)

9 letters
Magdalena (River)

10 letters
bullfights
campesinos (rural people)

12 letters
Barranquilla (seaport)

CROSSING OVER

DIRECTIONS

Use a pencil for this game. Find words from the following list (the words not in parentheses) that have the correct number of spaces and letters to fit into the crossing-over boxes. Each word has a place where it belongs. The first word is done for you. To continue, find an 8-letter word with a "b" in the sixth space, and so on. All the words tell about Colombia.

3 letters
bus (important transportation)
(natural) **gas**

4 letters
coal
(coastal Indians) **fish**
corn
(much) **gold**
(much) **salt**
rice
(sugar-water drink) **agua** (de panela)

5 letters
Andes (Mountains)
Cauca (River)
(Cristóbal) **Colón** (mountain peak)
(many small) **farms**
sugar (cane)

Village

Name _____ Date _____

NUMBER CODE

DIRECTIONS

Look at the number under each line. Find the matching number in the code box. Write the letters that matches that number on the answer line.

A - 1	G - 7	M - 13	S - 19	Y - 25
B - 2	H - 8	N - 14	T - 20	Z - 26
C - 3	I - 9	O - 15	U - 21	
D - 4	J - 10	P - 16	V - 22	
E - 5	K - 11	Q - 17	W - 23	
F - 6	L - 12	R - 18	X - 24	

1. What does Peru have?
   __1__ __4__ __5__ __19__ __5__ __18__ __20__ __4__ __18__ __9__ __5__ __18__ __20__ __8__ __1__ __14__
   __20__ __8__ __5__ __19__ __1__ __8__ __1__ __18__ __1__

2. The ruins of Machu Picchu were once
   __1__ __23__ __1__ __12__ __12__ __5__ __4__ __9__ __14__ __3__ __1__
   __3__ __9__ __20__ __25__ .

Boat with Palm-thatched Roof

3. What's special about the Andes Mountains?
   __20__ __8__ __5__ __1__ __9__ __18__ __9__ __19__
   __3__ __18__ __25__ __19__ __20__ __1__ __12__ __3__ __12__ __5__ __1__ __18__ .

4. In what is Peru a world leader?
   __16__ __18__ __15__ __4__ __21__ __3__ __9__ __14__ __7__ __3__ __15__ __16__ __16__ __5__ __18__ ,
   __12__ __5__ __1__ __4__ , __19__ __9__ __12__ __22__ __5__ __18__ __1__ __14__ __4__ __26__ __9__ __14__ __3__

5. What is Peru's capital?
   __12__ __9__ __13__ __1__

6. What ancient ruins are in Chanchan?
   __20__ __8__ __5__ __3__ __8__ __9__ __13__ __21__ __9__ __14__ __4__ __9__ __1__ __14__ __19__ ,
   __3__ __1__ __16__ __9__ __20__ __1__ __12__

7. Many of the Peruvian Indians' ancestors were the
   __9__ __14__ __3__ __1__ __19__ .

8. Today, one of the official languages is
   __17__ __21__ __5__ __3__ __8__ __21__ , __1__ __14__ __9__ __14__ __3__ __1__
   __12__ __1__ __14__ __7__ __21__ __1__ __7__ __5__ .

9. Peru has
   __5__ __1__ __18__ __20__ __8__ __17__ __21__ __1__ __11__ __5__ __19__ .

10. Lake __20__ __9__ __20__ __9__ __3__ __1__ __3__ __1__ is the world's largest navigable lake.

11. At one time, wild __16__ __15__ __20__ __1__ __20__ __15__ __5__ __19__ only grew in Peru's highlands.

12. The Indians graze mostly sheep and __12__ __12__ __1__ __13__ __1__ __19__ in the highland valleys.

Getting Water

148

VENEZUELA SOUTH AMERICA

Name _____ Date _____

NAME THE LARGE SEAPORT AND CITY

DIRECTIONS

Fill in the dotted lines with your answers. If they are correct, the circled letters will spell the name of a large seaport and city in Venezuela.

1. A world leader in producing this mineral
2. Traditional bread (corn meal cakes)
3. Capital and largest city
4. Immense plains (name of one of four land regions)
5. Famous cave with thousands of birds living in it: Cave of the _____
6. Country that once ruled
7. One of the world's largest dams
8. Important meat
9. All of Venezuela is in the _____ zone.

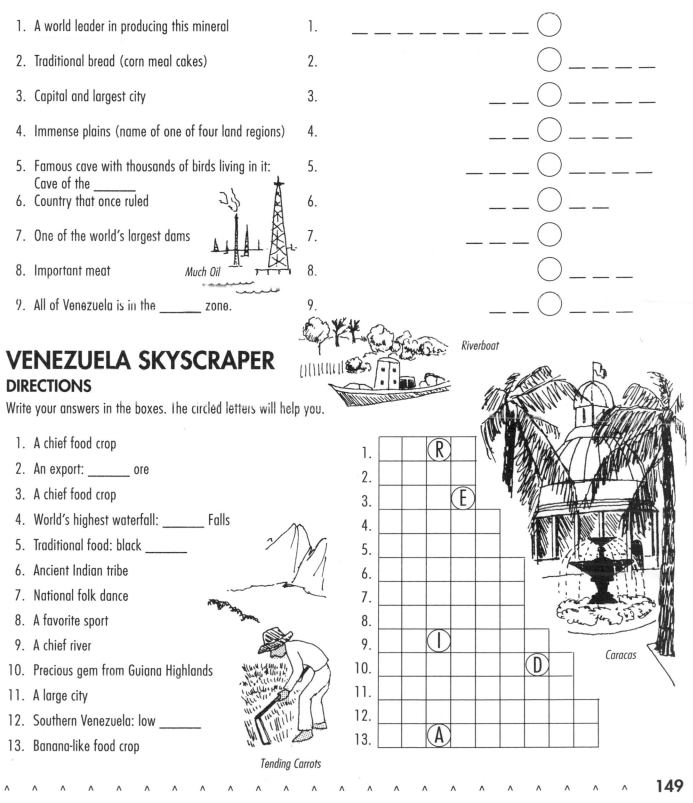

Much Oil

Riverboat

Caracas

VENEZUELA SKYSCRAPER

DIRECTIONS

Write your answers in the boxes. The circled letters will help you.

1. A chief food crop
2. An export: _____ ore
3. A chief food crop
4. World's highest waterfall: _____ Falls
5. Traditional food: black _____
6. Ancient Indian tribe
7. National folk dance
8. A favorite sport
9. A chief river
10. Precious gem from Guiana Highlands
11. A large city
12. Southern Venezuela: low _____
13. Banana-like food crop

Tending Carrots

ANSWER KEY

AFRICA

3

NORTHERN-AREA COUNTRIES

4

NORTHERN-AREA CAPITALS

5

CENTRAL-AREA COUNTRIES

6

CENTRAL-AREA CAPITALS

7

SOUTHERN-AREA COUNTRIES

8

SOUTHERN-AREA CAPITALS

9

ALGERIA

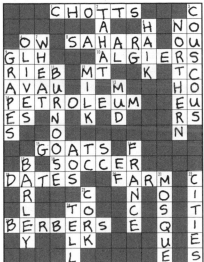

10

EGYPT

12

LIBERIA

15

CONGO NAME THE CITY

1. **B** ananas
2. pet **R** oleum
3. c **A** noe
4. **Z** aire
5. Bra **Z** zaville
6. **A** tlantic
7. **V** alley
8. hum **I** d
9. **L** umber
10. oi **L**
11. **E** quator

CONGO CLUE

Some chief crops:
  peanuts
  rice
  rubber
  sugar cane
Chief river:
  Congo
Northern Congo has:
  forests
Official language:
  French
Some chief crops:
  cassava
  palm oil
  plantains
  yams
  sweet potatoes
Import port:
  Pointe Noire
A French explorer:
  Brazza
A famous British explorer on the Congo River:
  Stanley

ETHIOPIA

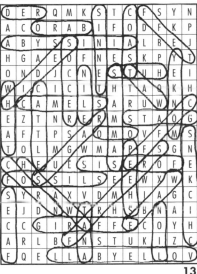

13

KENYA

14

MADAGASCAR NAME THE PIRATE WHO SAILED TO MADAGASCAR

1. **C** offee
2. v **A** nilla
3. sweet **P** otato
4. ca **T** tle
5. Ant **A** nanarivo
6. sh **I** ps
7. Fran **N** ce
8. mar **K** et
9. r **I** ce
10. her **D** ers
11. hi **D** es

MADAGASCAR SCRAMBLED WORDS

1. lemur
2. cloves
3. Africa
4. Indonesia
5. Mozambique

16

NIGERIA

17

ZAIRE

(crossword grid)

20

TREES AND PLANTS

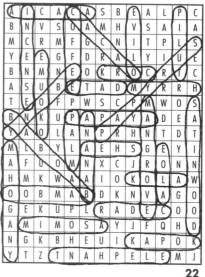

22

SOUTH AFRICA

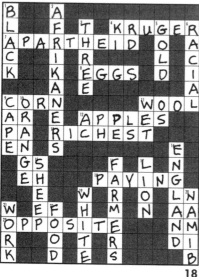

18

SAHARA DESERT CLUE

Oasis crops:
  dates
  barley
  wheat
Desert animals:
  gerbils
  snakes
  sheep
  gazelles
Occasionally seen on mountain peaks:
  snow
Rain:
  some areas, less than one inch per year
Nights are:
  cool
Sometimes, 600 feet high:
  dunes
  Some plants only last six or eight weeks
Once crossed the desert on trading routes:
  caravans
  In ancient times, there were farms and people fished

SAHARA DESERT SKYSCRAPER

1. U.S.
2. oil
3. ergs
4. oases
5. camels
6. largest
7. Atlantic
8. mountains
9. Mauritania
10. underground

21

UGANDA NUMBER CODE

1. Victoria Lake
2. Kampala
3. Farm, and women do a lot of the work
4. Grassland with low trees
5. High plateau and mild temperatures
6. Bananas, beans, cassava, corn, millet, sweet potatoes
7. Coffee, cotton, sugar cane; tea is most important

19

WILD ANIMALS

23

EXPORTS

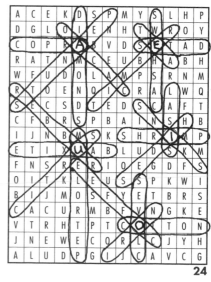

24

152

CHIEF FARM PRODUCTS

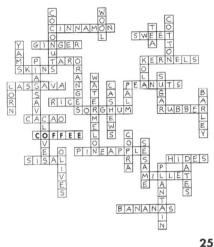

25

INTERESTING FACTS NUMBER CODE (BENIN THROUGH GAMBIA)

1. bamboo huts built on stakes above the water
2. about 10,000 bushmen, with yellow-brown skin, still hunt with bows and arrows
3. some people are pygmies (small people)
4. famous for mask and statue-making
5. tsetse fly—causes sleeping sickness
6. a perfume comes from the ylang-ylang tree
7. travel in dugout canoes
8. was once a slave-trading center

26

INTERESTING FACTS NUMBER CODE (KENYA THROUGH TANZANIA)

1. world-famous for its wild animals
2. founded by some American as a home for freed slaves
3. was once a favorite base for sea pirates
4. slum-home areas built with tin cans
5. "tent schools" follow nomadic tribes
6. giant tortoises; double coconuts weigh about
7. diamonds found in swamps and riverbeds
8. Kilimanjaro

27

MOUNTAINS

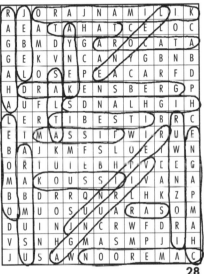

28

RIVERS

29

FISHING AND FAVORITE FOODS NUMBER CODE

anchovies
carp   mackerel
hake   perch
sardines   shad
sardinella   shrimp
tuna   rock lobster

1. couscous (steamed wheat or barley with meat, vegetables, sauce)
2. felafel (vegetables, flour, spices, sauce, served in pita bread)
3. chicken stew; spicy meat or fish with peanut sauce
4. wat (a stew)

30

DESERTS, LAKES, SPECIAL AREAS

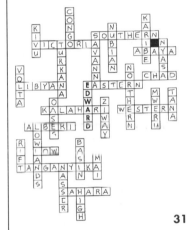

31

SEAPORTS

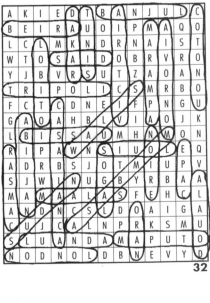

32

NAMES OF CLOTHING NUMBER CODE

1. shammas
2. kenti cloth
3. fez   djellaba   caftans
4. sari
5. galabiyah
6. taub
7. boubou
8. burnoose   haik
9. lappa
10. lungi   toga

33

LATITUDE AND LONGITUDE A THROUGH L

1. Algeria
2. Benin
3. Burkina Faso
4. Cameroon
5. Central African Republic
6. Comoros
7. Djibouti
8. Equatorial Guinea
9. Gambia
10. Guinea
11. Ivory Coast
12. Lesotho
13. Libya
14. Angola
15. Botswana
16. Burundi
17. Cape Verde
18. Chad
19. Congo
20. Egypt
21. Gabon
22. Ghana
23. Guinea-Bissau
24. Kenya
25. Liberia

34

LATITUDE AND LONGITUDE M THROUGH Z

1. Madagascar
2. Mali
3. Mauritius
4. Mozambique
5. Nigeria
6. São Tomé and Príncipe
7. Seychelles
8. Somalia
9. Sudan
10. Tanzania
11. Tunisia
12. Zaire
13. Zimbabwe
14. Malawi
15. Mauritania
16. Morocco
17. Niger
18. Rwanda
19. Senegal
20. Sierra Leone
21. South Africa
22. Swaziland
23. Togo
24. Uganda
25. Zambia

35

ANTARCTICA

37

ASIA

39

INDEPENDENT COUNTRIES A THROUGH L

40

From *The Continents*, published by GoodYearBooks. Copyright © 1994 Jeanne and Arnold Cheyney.

CAPITALS OF INDEPENDENT COUNTRIES A THROUGH L

41

INDEPENDENT COUNTRIES L THROUGH Y

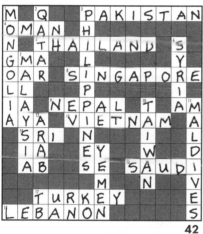

42

CAPITALS OF INDEPENDENT COUNTRIES L THROUGH Y

43

WILD ANIMALS

44

CROPS

45

TREES AND PLANTS

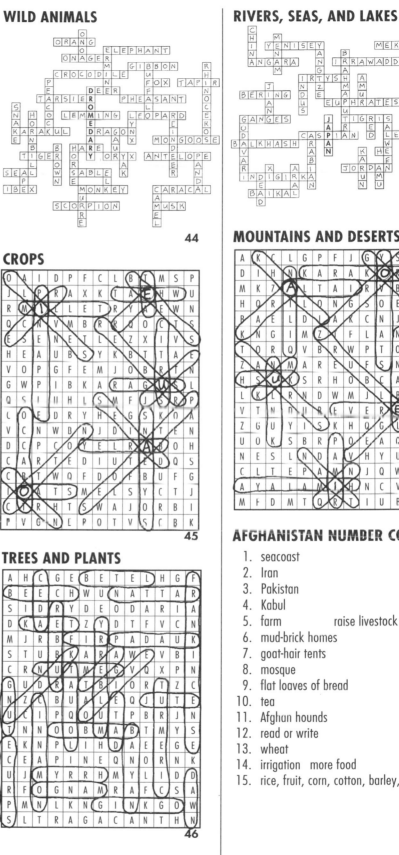

46

RIVERS, SEAS, AND LAKES

47

MOUNTAINS AND DESERTS

48

AFGHANISTAN NUMBER CODE

1. seacoast
2. Iran
3. Pakistan
4. Kabul
5. farm   raise livestock
6. mud-brick homes
7. goat-hair tents
8. mosque
9. flat loaves of bread
10. tea
11. Afghan hounds
12. read or write
13. wheat
14. irrigation   more food
15. rice, fruit, corn, cotton, barley, nuts

49

From *The Continents*, published by GoodYearBooks. Copyright © 1994 Jeanne and Arnold Cheyney.

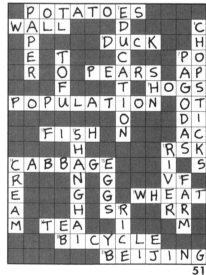

BURMA NAME AN IMPORTANT RIVER

1. r I verboat
2. R angoon
3. R ead
4. f A rmers
5. teak W ood
6. b A mboo
7. floo D s
8. ja D e
9. M ay

BURMA PAIRS OF CROPS AND FOODS

onions garlic
vegetables fruit
sugar wheat
jute cotton
peanuts sesame
corn millet
tobacco rubber
fish shrimp
chicken bananas
citrus durians
chief crop
  rice   50

CHINA

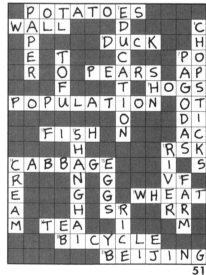

51

HONG KONG AND SRI LANKA NUMBER CODE

1. a British dependency, leased from China until
2. Victoria
3. an international trade center, with many banks
4. Chinese
5. tourists semitropical mountains hills
6. Ceylon India
7. Colombo
8. farmers
9. tea, rubber, spices, rubies, sapphires, rice, cassava
10. read write

52

INDIA

53

IRAN

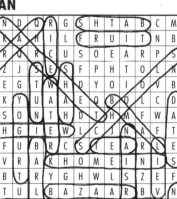

54

IRAQ NAME THE RIVER

1. cam E l
2. k U rds
3. shee P
4. B a g H dad
5. Tig R is
6. f A rmers
7. deser T
8. E l Bashah
9. brick S

IRAQ SCRAMBLED CROPS

1. dates
2. melons
3. wheat
4. oats
5. barley
6. olives
7. fruit
8. rice
9. tomatoes

IRAQ WORDS IN WORDS

late wrote leaf loafer wore
fate rote beef turf roar
seat rate seal surf safe
feet tear lease fret safer
beat fear about sole were
beet leer least role rear
buffet wear feast waffle stow
sofa bear stew soufflé swat
base seer brew baffle affable
abuse bustle slew raffle able
waste beau also toffee table
fare feel buffer sore sable
boat reel suffer soar fable
float real loaf tore

55

ISRAEL

Crossword grid answers include: A V I V, I, D, MILK, JERUSALEM, HOLY, FERTILE, MELONS, HOT, ADVANCED, JESUS, SALT, HEBREW, CITRUS

(down/across words partially visible: ARABS, NEGEV, ISRAEL, FLOWER, JORDAN, etc.)

56

MALAYSIA

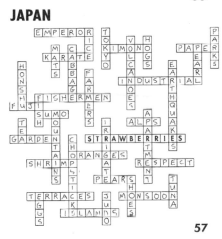

Word search grid:

```
O W T A K L G R E B B U R
I H R A I N T Y N O B E I
E D O K N W B M F A O N Q
L X P G G S Y S A C S V T
E C I R C G B G N A H A P
P F C D J N J N E C R P S
H E A R C O I O S M I M U
A H L U M P U R G F M O Q
N F G P L M K A I R P N R
T K V E U A T S P U S K A
W A Y P Z K H R T I G E R
K R A P P U P P E T B Y B
V E G E T A B L E S F C O
R P J R E L I D O C O R C
E A D R A Z I L D E X I G
E L P P A E N I P L E H M
D M A N G R O V E O N S N
```

59

JAPAN

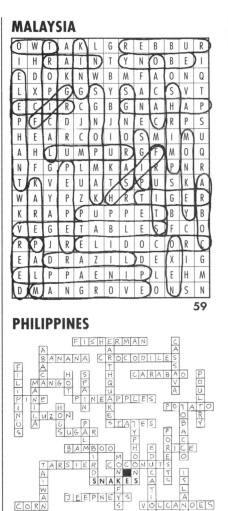

Crossword answers include: EMPEROR, KIMONOS, PAPER, PARKS, KARATE, INDUSTRIAL, FISHERMEN, SUMO, ALPS, GARDEN, STRAWBERRIES, ORANGES, RESPECT, SHRIMP, PEARS, TUNA, TERRACES, MONSOON, ISLANDS, HONSHU, FUJI, EARTHQUAKE

57

KUWAIT NUMBER CODE

1. Iraq   Saudi Arabia
2. a world leader in petroleum production
3. world's richest countries
4. education, health service, no income tax
5. Hawalli
6. Emir
7. Persian Gulf
8. hot   April   September
9. rivers
10. distilled ocean water
11. turning desert into farmland by irrigation
12. American   British   oil

58

PHILIPPINES

Crossword answers include: FISHERMAN, BANANA, CROCODILES, CARABAO, MANGO, PINEAPPLES, POTATO, POULTRY, LUZON, STATES, SUGAR, BAMBOO, RICE, TARSIER, COCONUTS, SNAKES, JEEPNEYS, VOLCANOES, CORN, FILIPINOS

60

SAUDI ARABIA NAME THE SOURCE OF WEALTH

1.   P eople
2.   o a s E s
3. d e s e r T
4.   R iyadh
5.   s c h O o l s
6.   t e L evision
7.   B E douins
8.   T a n U r a
9.   s h r i M p

SAUDI ARABIA SCRAMBLED FOODS

1. rice
2. fruits
3. dates
4. meat
5. lamb
6. wheat
7. vegetables
8. milk
9. cheese
10. coffee

SAUDI ARABIA WORDS IN WORDS

rain	sour	snout	mist	hush
stain	roust	rout	insist	mush
main	roast	shout	mash	noun
mount	toast	mast	rash	mountain
sham	astir	harm	hash	train
mitt	tint	taint	sash	human
stair	hint	saint	rush	

61

SOUTH KOREA NAME AN IMPORTANT FISH

1.   **F** r e e d o m
2.   **R** **I** c e
3.   S e o u **L**
4.   t w **E** n t y
5.   **F** o r e s t s
6.   K **I** m c h i
7.   m o n **S** o o n
8.   t y p **H** o o n

SOUTH KOREA SKYSCRAPER

1. own
2. hog
3. Han
4. fish
5. eggs
6. elect
7. apple
8. onion
9. barley
10. Naktong
11. economies   62

SYRIA

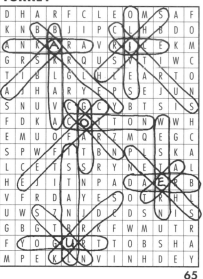

63

TAIWAN NUMBER CODE

1. Formosa
2. Thick forests
3. Taipei
4. Mountain rivers
5. hot and humid
6. Typhoons
7. Bus: excellent transportation
8. pointed straw hats
9. rice, tea, asparagus, citrus fruits, mushrooms, peanuts, vegetables, corn, pineapple
10. can read and write   64

TURKEY

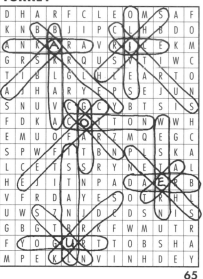

65

VIETNAM NAME THE COUNTRIES THAT ONCE RULED

1.   **F** i s h e r m e n
2.   f o **R** e s t s
3.   H **A** n o i
4.   C h i **N** a
5.   r i **C** e
6.   t i r **E** s

1.   **J** u t e
2.   f **A** r m
3.   t r o **P** i c a l
4.   f **A** r m e r s
5.   H o C h i M i **N** h C i t y

VIETNAM SKYSCRAPER

1. tea
2. Red
3. fish
4. Annam
5. cassava
6. peanuts
7. potatoes
8. coconuts   66

AUSTRALIA

STATES, MAINLAND TERRITORIES, AND CAPITALS

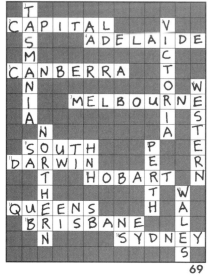

69

AUSTRALIA

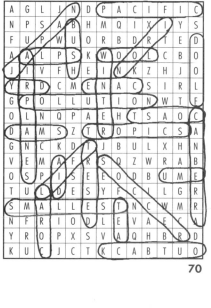

70

From *The Continents*, published by GoodYearBooks. Copyright © 1994 Jeanne and Arnold Cheyney.

NEW ZEALAND

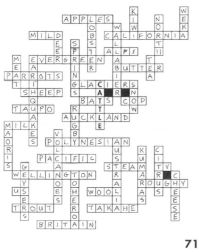

71

EUROPE

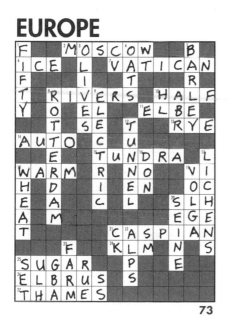

73

NORTHERN-AREA COUNTRIES

74

NORTHERN-AREA CAPITALS

75

SOUTHERN-AREA COUNTRIES

76

SOUTHERN-AREA CAPITALS

77

COMMONWEALTH OF INDEPENDENT STATES

78

CAPITALS OF COMMONWEALTH OF INDEPENDENT STATES

79

BIRDS AND ANIMALS

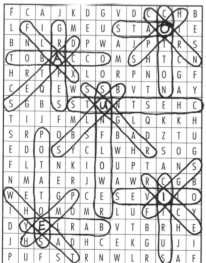

```
N E T R A M C B E G R E T
D L E B R M L E M M I N G
G K H E L C H A M O I S O
A I T I B B A R N X P S H
F T K J O O N I B O R T E
O W L R A T Y S Q F R O G
U E D V R E I N D E E R R
F L O W C P I J W A B K E
Z E G L K W I F T G H Y H
Q R N S P I U G V U L L T
M R S E O L W A E E O A X
L I Z A R D Q E W O A X Z
B U F L K C J N P S C Z H
G Q C S B A D G E R N J C
L S H M I T H Y G O F M N
I E D R W O R R A P S K I
N I G H T I N G A L E L F
```
80

CROPS

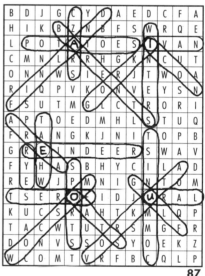

```
F C A J K D G V D C C H B
L F I G M E U S T A X E
B N L R D W A P R J I H
T O B A C C O M S H T C N
H R T P X L O R P N O G F
C E Q E W S S B V T N J
S G B S S T U N T S E H C
T I J F M L N G L Q K K H
S R P O B S F B A D Z T U
E D O S Y C L W H R S O G
F L T N K I O U P T A N S
N M A E R J W A W R C G B
W E T G P C E S E V I O
I H O M O M R L U F Y R Y
D H S A D H C E K G U J I
P U F S T R N W L R S A F
```
81

EUROPE RIVER PAIRS

Don	Rhine	Danube	Loire
Dnepr	Neman	Dvina	Oder
Vistula	Elbe	Po	Rhone
Seine	Tagus	Ebro	Thames
Garonne	Prut	Donets	Mezen
Dnestr	Kama	Pechora	

Longest river: Volga

82

SEAS NUMBER CODE

1. Barents
2. Norwegian
3. Baltic
4. North
5. Mediterranean
6. Black
7. Aegean
8. Adriatic   **83**

AUSTRIA NAME THE POPULAR DISH

1.   **W** heat
2.   sk **I**
3.   for **E** sts
4.   coastli **N** e
5.   cak **E**
6.   cultu **R** al

7.   spa **S**
8.   **C** halets
9.   sc **H** illing
10.   sce **N** ery
11.   cur **I** Ing
12. presiden **T**
13.   Mo **Z** art
14.   **E** ggs
15.   sa **L** t

AUSTRIA SCRAMBLED WORDS

1. mountains
2. Vienna
3. dairy
4. German
5. sugar beets
6. livestock
7. corn   **84**

BELGIUM

85

COMMONWEALTH OF INDEPENDENT STATES (FORMERLY U.S.S.R.) NUMBER CODE

1. Iran   Aras R.
2. of Caspian Sea
3. Poland
4. South   Russia
5. China
6. Romania   Prut River
7. Kazakhstan
8. China
9. Iran
10. Poland
11. Aral Sea
12. Finland
13. Black
14. Baltic
15. Baltic   **86**

COMMONWEALTH OF INDEPENDENT STATES RUSSIA

```
B D J G C Y D A E D C F A
H I K B Z N B F S W R Q E
L P O T A O E S I V A N
C M N L R R H S N C U K A
O N N W A S E R J T W O A
R I Q P V K O N V E Y S N
F S U T M G L C T R O R I
A P T O E D M H L S T U Q
F R A N G K J N I T O P B
G R E I N D E E R S W A V
F Y H A S B H Y C I L A D
R E W J P M N I G N T O M
T S E R O I D I U R A L
K U C S R A H T K M L Q P
T A C W T U T R S M G F R
D O N V S S O S Y O E K Z
W C O M T V R F B C Q L P
```
87

From *The Continents*, published by GoodYearBooks. Copyright © 1994 Jeanne and Arnold Cheyney.

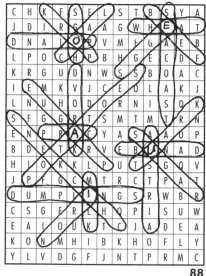

THE CZECH AND THE SLOVAK REPUBLICS

88

DENMARK

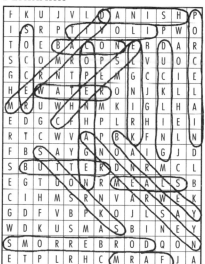

89

FINLAND NAME A CHIEF INDUSTRY

1. Wheat
2. thOusands
3. sOuthern
4. MiDnight Sun
5. Wood pulp
6. fOrests
7. TundRa
8. HelsinKi
9. Ice breakers
10. sauNa
11. suGar beets

FINLAND SKYSCRAPER

1. rye
2. oats
3. pine
4. fish
5. eggs
6. barley
7. butter
8. Sweden
9. Kemijoke
10. reindeer
11. computers
12. television

90

FRANCE

91

GERMANY

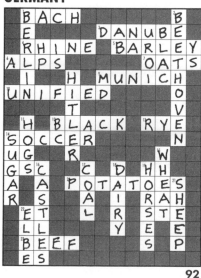

92

GREAT BRITAIN (ENGLAND AND WALES)

93

GREAT BRITAIN (SCOTLAND AND NORTHERN IRELAND)

94

GREECE NUMBER CODE

1. Athens
2. islands
3. largest merchant fleets
4. alpha   beta   alphabet
5. olympic games were held in Greece
6. mountains cover most of Greece
7. lemons olives   raisins
8. bouzoukis
9. Parthenon
10. coffee   houses
11. lamb
12. olive oil
13. moussaka

95

From *The Continents*, published by GoodYearBooks. Copyright © 1994 Jeanne and Arnold Cheyney.

ICELAND

96

IRELAND WHAT IS IRELAND SOMETIMES CALLED?

1. famin E
2. far M
3. p E at
4. P a t R ick
5. pot A toes
6. Dub L in
7. brea D

8. Celt I c
9. S h a n n o n
10. fo L k
11. Gr E at

IRELAND SKYSCRAPER

1. pub
2. cod
3. hay
4. stew
5. Mayo
6. milk
7. sheep
8. pasture
9. chicken
10. divorce
11. mackerel
12. instrument   97

ITALY

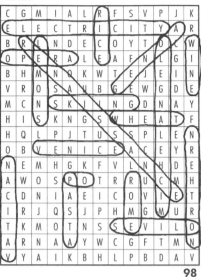

98

NETHERLANDS

99

NORWAY NAME THE FAVORITE SANDWICH SPREAD

1. midni G ht
2. fi O rds
3. me A ls
4. indus T ries

5. s C hool
6. H erring
7. E lectric
8. p E troleum
9. S kiing
10. ic E free

NORWAY SKYSCRAPER

1. hay
2. king
3. Oslo
4. fish
5. Lapps
6. Arctic
7. vikings
8. minister
9. livestock
10. ombudsman
11. Scandianavian   100

SPAIN

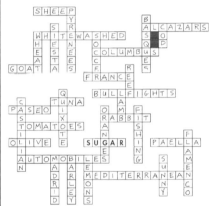

101

SWEDEN

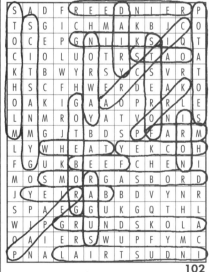

102

From *The Continents*, published by GoodYearBooks. Copyright © 1994 Jeanne and Arnold Cheyney.

SWITZERLAND NUMBER CODE

1. watches, cheese, chocolates
2. banking
3. Bern
4. Zurich
5. neutral in European wars   citizens' army   militia   take training
6. Johanna Spyri wrote Heidi;   Wyss family wrote   Swiss Family Robinson
7. Swiss alps
8. Matterhorn   border
9. skiing, climbing, bobsledding, hiking, bicycling

103

NORTH AMERICA

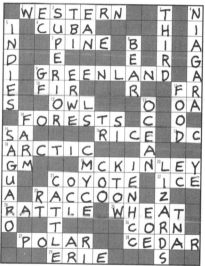

105

INDEPENDENT COUNTRIES

106

CAPITALS OF INDEPENDENT COUNTRIES

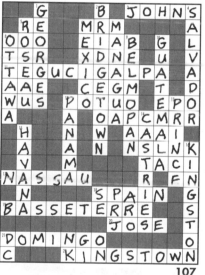

107

ISLAND: POLITICAL UNITS

108

ISLAND: CAPITALS OF POLITICAL UNITS

109

FARM PRODUCTS

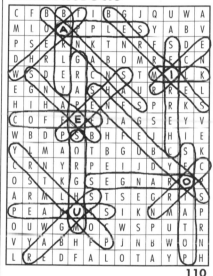

110

LAKES

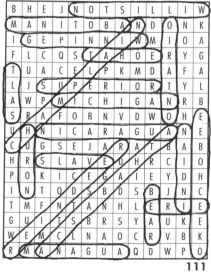

111

RIVERS

112

TREES

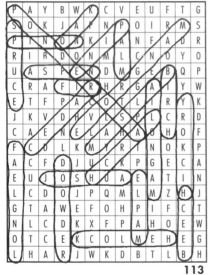

113

WILD ANIMALS

114

CANADA PROVINCES, TERRITORIES, ABBREVIATIONS

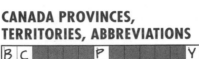

115

CANADA CAPITALS

116

CANADA NAME SOMETHING SPECIAL ABOUT CANADA

1. OttaWa
2. tOtem
3. ARctic
4. poLar bears
5. Dikes
6. houSes
7. Snakes
8. QuEbec
9. provinCes
10. snOwmobiles
11. maNnufacturing
12. GranD Banks
13. bottLes
14. skAting
15. NoRth Atlantic
16. aGricultural
17. QuEbec City
18. BritiSh Columbia
19. WhiTehorse
20. Caribou
21. mOtorboats
22. hoUr
23. Newfoundland
24. Trees
25. fuR
26. Yellowknife

117

CANADA

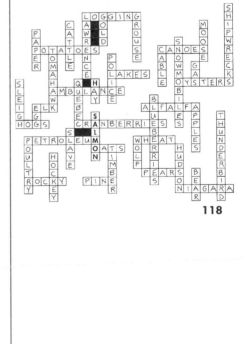

118

164

CENTRAL AMERICA

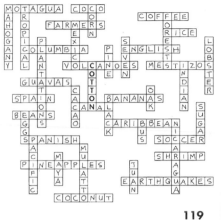

119

GREENLAND NAME SOMETHING SPECIAL ABOUT GREENLAND

1. NorWay
2. cOld
3. enmaRk
4. seaLs
5. CanaDa
6. ESkimos

7. poLar
8. wAter
9. militaRy
10. Godthab
11. lakE
12. potatoeS
13. midnighT

14. fIords
15. Sheep
16. gLaciers
17. hAy
18. fishiNg
19. coD

120

MEXICO FOOD PAIRS

tamales (meat and peppers in cornmeal dough, wrapped in cornhusk and steamed)
atole (thick corn-meal soup)
frijoles (beans, fried, mashed, refried)
tostados (tortilla fried crisp, topped with cheese, meat, vegetables)
enchiladas (spicy meat or cheese rolled in a tortilla, with chili sauce)

tacos	corn
beans	onions
tomatoes	bananas
mangoes (fruit)	oranges
papayas (fruit)	honey
squash	potatoes (sweet)
chocolate (hot)	avocados (fruit)

tortillas (thin, round cornmeal cakes)

rice

MEXICO SKYSCRAPER

1. Rio
2. Spain
3. Texas
4. Aztec
5. plaza
6. patios
7. silver
8. coffee
9. turkey
10. fiesta
11. piñata
12. sombrero
13. mariachis
14. bullfighting

121

WEST INDIES NUMBER CODE

1. foods
2. planes fly
3. ferries sail
4. painted pastel colors
   storm shutters on windows
5. volcanoes
6. tropical
7. Hurricanes sometimes hit.
8. very blue and beautiful
9. poor farmers huts
10. beans, crabs, fish, rice, sweet potatoes, bananas, mangoes, oranges
11. music, soccer, cockfights, baseball, basketball, cricket

122

UNITED STATES EASTERN-AREA STATES

123

UNITED STATES EASTERN-AREA CAPITALS

124

UNITED STATES CENTRAL-AREA STATES

125

UNITED STATES CENTRAL-AREA STATE CAPITALS

126

UNITED STATES WESTERN-AREA STATES

127

UNITED STATES WESTERN-AREA STATE CAPITALS

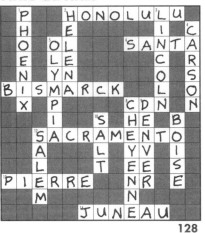

128

UNITED STATES NAME THE AMERICAN INVENTION

1. forEst
2. Largest
3. fErtile
4. PaCific
5. Telephone
6. Rockies
7. MIchigan
8. AtlantiC

9. AnnapoLis
10. DIsneyland
11. NiaGara
12. Helen Keller
13. DeaTh Valley

14. Buffalo
15. HUron
16. EvergLades
17. Boonesborough

129

UNITED STATES CROSSING OVER

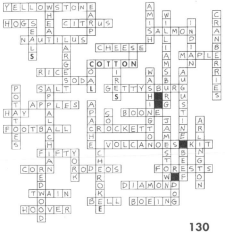

130

ALASKA

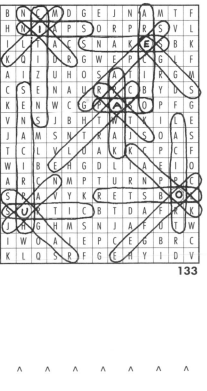

131

HAWAII NUMBER CODE

1. southwest
2. mild all year
3. Honolulu
4. Polynesians
5. youngest U.S. state
6. Pacific Military Command Base
7. twelve letters
   (A E H I K L M N O P U W)
8. active volcanoes
9. Haleakala Crater
10. water sports
11. luau, hula, ukulele, lei
12. pineapples grow
13. taro, guavas, bananas

132

PUERTO RICO

133

From *The Continents*, published by GoodYearBooks. Copyright © 1994 Jeanne and Arnold Cheyney.

SOUTH AMERICA

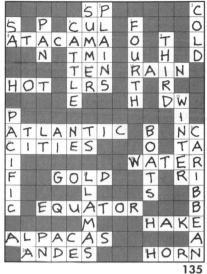

135

INDEPENDENT COUNTRIES AND POLITICAL UNITS

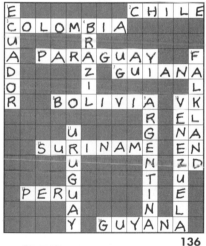

136

CAPITALS OF INDEPENDENT COUNTRIES AND POLITICAL UNITS

137

FISHING CATCHES, RIVERS, OCEANS, SEAS, AND WATERFALLS

138

TREES, PLANTS, FLOWERS

139

ANIMALS

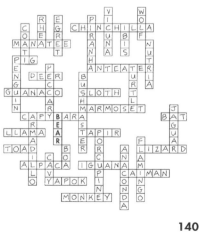

140

MOUNTAINS, DAMS, LAKES, AND DESERTS

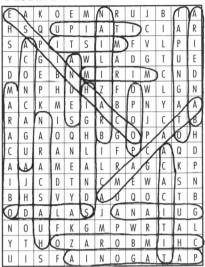

141

LATITUDE AND LONGITUDE

1. Brazil
2. Argentina
3. Ecuador
4. Chile
5. Venezuela
6. Uruguay
7. Bolivia
8. Guyana
9. Peru
10. Paraguay
11. Suriname
12. Colombia
13. French Guiana

THINGS OF INTEREST NUMBER CODE

1. Antarctica
2. two capitals
3. plants, trees, birds
4. fishing industries
5. auto races, bullfights
6. volcano
7. below sea level
8. cars
9. Machu Picchu   Inca city
10. trees
11. barbecued sausage, beef
12. Little Venice

143

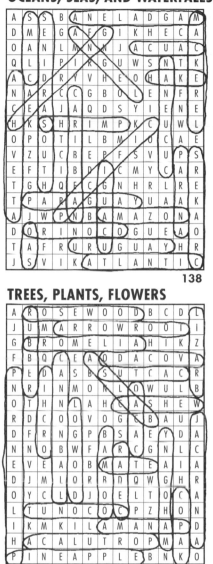

FARM PRODUCTS

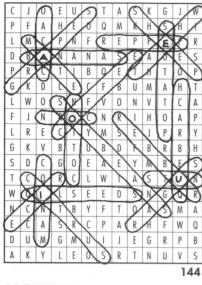

```
C J O E U S T A S K G J W
P F A H E O Q M K H S H I
L M C P N F R E P E P E R
D B A N A N A S E A O E S
P R C T I B O E T H T O P
G K D C E C F B U M A H T
L W O S N F V O N V T C A
F J N X O C N R I H O A P
L R E C I Y M S E J P R Y
G C K V B T U B D F B R H
S D C G O E A E Y M B E S
T C O R C L W I A S X U N
W O I L S E E D S N G Q R
N C N T B Y F T O A S M A
E C A S R C P A R H F W Q
D U M G M U I J E G R P B
A K Y L E O S R T N U V S
```
144

ARGENTINA

```
¹TEA      ³C    ⁴PAMPA
²MESTIZOS
     L    R    ⁶P
⁷WHEAT    N    ⁸ANDES
⁹CATTLE  ¹⁰GAUCHO
     A         ¹¹I
¹²SOCCER  WOOL  L
     A    CANE ¹³MS
¹⁴FORESTS  I    E
     N   ¹⁵FLAX A
   ¹⁶HIDES    ²⁰PATO
     V        ²¹S
²²SPAIN   ²³BUENOS
²⁵MILK    EN   I
     ²⁶MATE  ²⁷GOLD
²⁸IGUACO  F
```
146

BRAZIL

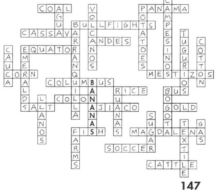

```
RIO
LEMONS    GAUCHOS
   HALF        TROPICS
   BEANS
      BUTTERFLIES
   NORDESTINOS    ORANGE
              CARNAUBA
COFFEE     IGUACU
        PORTUGUESE
              SOIL
   BRASILIA  PARANA
   COTTON
```
146

COLOMBIA

```
COAL        PANAMA
CASSAVA  BULLFIGHTS
EQUATOR  ANDES
CORN
   COLUMBUS    MESTIZOS
   COLON  RICE    GOLD
   SALT  AJIACO
LLANOS
   FISH  MAGDALENA
      SOCCER
         CATTLE
```
147

PERU NUMBER CODE

1. a desert drier than the Sahara
2. a walled Inca city
3. The air is crystal clear.
4. producing copper, lead, silver and zinc
5. Lima
6. the Chimu Indians' capital
7. Incas
8. Quechua, an Inca language
9. earthquakes
10. Titicaca
11. potatoes
12. llamas

148

VENEZUELA NAME THE LARGE SEAPORT AND CITY

1. petroleuM
2.   Arepa
3. CaRacas
4. LlAnos
5. GuaCharo
6. SpAin
7. GurI
8.   Beef
9. trOpic

VENEZUELA SKYSCRAPER

1. corn
2. iron
3. rice
4. Angel
5. beans
6. Caribs
7. joropo
8. soccer
9. Orinoco
10. diamonds
11. Valencia
12. mountains
13. plantains

149

From *The Continents*, published by GoodYearBooks. Copyright © 1994 Jeanne and Arnold Cheyney.